LOOK 4

Rob Sved

COURSE CONSULTANTS

Paul Dummett

Elaine Boyd

NATIONAL GEOGRAPHIC
LEARNING

Australia • Brazil • Mexico • Singapore • United Kingdom • United States

Contents

		Words	**Grammar**	**Skills**
7 **Life in the past** p. 69		*the back, downstairs, entrance, floor, the front, gate, key, lift, roof, upstairs* Reading: *chalk, circle, glass, pavement, squares*	*Last week, we talked about the pyramids.* *They went to bed early in the evening.* *Today, children have to be careful.* *You had to draw squares on the pavement.*	Listen and learn about houses in ancient Egypt. Read about games children played outside. Write a timeline. Learn and speak about life today and in the past. **VALUE** Play outside.
8 **Fresh food** p. 77		*broccoli, cereal, chilli, sweetcorn, courgette jam, lettuce, nuts, olives, strawberry* Reading: *fresh food, junk food, seeds, weeds*	*How many chillies are there?* *How much cereal do you have for breakfast?* *Are there any vegetables?* *There is some water.* *They ate a few olives/a little fresh food.* *They grew lots of courgettes/lots of fresh food.*	Listen and learn about chillies. Read about the Community Vegetable Garden Project. Write a recipe. Learn and speak about food. **VALUE** Make your own food.

Game 2 p. 85   **Reading extra 2** The Wind and the Sun p. 86   **Review 4: Units 7–8** p. 88

9 **The world of the future** p. 89		*app, charge a tablet, e-book, go online, headphones, interactive whiteboard, laptop, microphone, VR headset, Wi-Fi* Reading: *control, drops, satellites, send a text*	*The robot will help a lot of students.* *They won't miss any lessons.* *One day, we'll have robots in our class.* *Will there be more drones in the future?* *Yes, there will./No, there won't.* *Where will they fly?*	Listen and learn about a school robot. Read about different uses of drones. Write an opinion text about the future. Learn and speak about technology now and in the future. **VALUE** Use your imagination.
10 **Feeling good!** p. 97		*asleep, awake, dark, dry, light, rest, strong, take exercise, weak, wet* Reading: *brush our teeth, shampoo, soap, toothbrush, toothpaste, towel*	*You should take some exercise.* *You shouldn't eat a lot before you sleep.* *Why do birds clean their feathers?* *Because it keeps them clean and strong.*	Listen and learn about sleep. Read about how animals keep clean. Write a message giving advice. Learn and speak about treating a cold. **VALUE** Sleep well.

Function 3 Requesting and offering help p. 105   School trip 3 Taking photos of lions p. 106   **Review 5: Units 9–10** p. 108

11 **City life** p. 109		*airport, bus station, chemist's, fire station, hotel, police station, railway station, restaurant, square, university* Reading: *chimneys, city centre, motorways, office blocks*	*He's been to Miniatur Wunderland.* *They haven't finished.* *Have you visited a big city?* *Yes, I have./No, I haven't.*	Listen and learn about Miniatur Wunderland. Read about Stephen Wiltshire's art. Write a poster about a city. Learn and speak about popular cities. **VALUE** Explore your city.
12 **You can do this!** p. 117		*crawl, discover, go gliding, go horseriding, go kayaking, go snorkelling, jump off, smell, swing, taste* Reading: *coast, hide, skills, splashed*	*Have you ever done something dangerous?* *Yes, I have./No, I haven't.* *She's seen a dolphin.* *Yesterday, I went snorkelling.*	Listen and learn about 125 challenges. Read about National Geographic Global Explorers. Write a survey and a survey report. Learn and speak about challenges. **VALUE** Challenge yourself.

Game 3 p. 125   **Reading extra 3** The man who wanted a simple life p. 126   **Review 6: Units 11–12** p. 128

Look further p. 129   **One more look** p. 129   BONUS **School trip** Hunting for fish p. 130
BONUS **Reading extra** Annie takes a challenge p. 132   **BONUS Game** p. 133

Camping in the evening, Yosemite, USA

Look and remember

1 Look at the photo. Tick (✓) the words you can see.

moon	☐	stars	☐
forest	☐	building	☐
picnic	☐	museum	☐
tent	☐	friends	☐
bat	☐	tree	☐
cloud	☐	skyscraper	☐

2 Read and complete the postcard.

Hi,

How are you? I'm ¹ *camping / camp* with my friends again this year. We always ² *coming / come* to this beautiful place. There ³ *are / aren't* many people so it's calm and quiet. At the moment, we're ⁴ *eating / eat* outside. We're having ⁵ *a / some* pasta and salad. Tomorrow we're going ⁶ *go / to go* canoeing and then we want to climb some trees in the forest.

See you soon!

3 Answer the questions. Then compare your answers in small groups.

1 Would you like to go camping here? Why? / Why not?
2 How often do you go camping?
3 What other activities do you like doing outside?

Look and remember

1 Look at the photo. Read and write T (true) or F (false).

1 There are two people in the photo.
2 The woman is wearing glasses.
3 The woman is angry.
4 The man is looking at the panda.
5 The man has got short hair.

2 Listen. Complete the information about giant pandas. 🎧 TR: 1

Giant Pandas

Number in China: [1]_____ giant pandas

Size at birth: [2]_____ centimetres long

Size of adults: taller than [3]_____ metre

Food: bamboo, for [4]_____ hours every day

Age: up to [5]_____ years old

3 Work in pairs. Choose another wild animal and write a factfile.

Animal: _____

Country/Countries: _____

How many: _____

Size: _____

Food: _____

How long they live: _____

4 Work with another pair. Ask and answer questions to guess each other's animal.

What does it eat?

It eats small animals.

The Bifengxia Giant Panda Research Center, Sichuan Province, China

Look and remember

1 **Write the odd one out.**

1 lake	river	waterfall	village	_____
2 pasta	bottle	plate	cup	_____
3 ant	dolphin	kangaroo	panda	_____
4 curly	straight	moustache	long	_____
5 neck	cough	shoulder	stomach	_____
6 son	daughter	sister	grandmother	_____

2 **Write two odd-one-out puzzles for your friend.**

1 _____   _____   _____   _____

2 _____   _____   _____   _____

3 **Write questions. Then ask and answer the questions in pairs.**

1 are / you / old / how

_____?

2 your / is / when / birthday

_____?

3 and sisters / got / brothers / any / you / have

_____?

4 Saturdays / you / do / on / what / usually / do

_____?

5 like / books / you / do / comic / reading

_____?

6 on Sunday / going to / you / what / do / are

_____?

4 **Think about your favourite things. Then ask and answer in small groups.**

animal   sport   food   place to visit   country   activity   fruit

What's your favourite animal?

A cat. What's yours?

All kinds of jobs

Burj Khalifa, Dubai

Look at the photo. Answer the questions.

1 Where is the man?

2 What is he doing? Why?

3 What does he need for his job?

4 Would you like this job? Why? / Why not?

9

1 **Listen and repeat.** 🎧 TR: 2

actor

clown

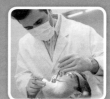
dentist

firefighter

nurse

photographer

pilot

police officer

waiter

2 **Answer the questions.**

1 Which jobs do people sometimes do outside?
2 Which jobs help other people?

3 **Listen to the conversation about smoke jumpers. Write T (true) or F (false).** 🎧 TR: 3

1 Smoke jumpers jump out of a plane as a hobby. ☐
2 A smoke jumper is a kind of firefighter. ☐
3 Smoke jumpers fight fires in forests all year. ☐
4 The smoke jumpers carry all the equipment when they jump. ☐
5 The smoke jumper in the photo is Russian. ☐
6 There are about 400 US smoke jumpers. ☐

Smoke jumpers are training in the US.

Grammar

1 **Listen and read.** 🎧 TR: 4

> **Present simple and present continuous**
>
> We use the present simple for things that we do all the time or that we do many times. We often use it with time expressions like *every day*, *on Mondays, once a week*.
>
> They *fight* fires in forests *every summer*.
>
> We use the present continuous to talk about things that are happening now. We often use it with time expressions like *now, at the moment, today*.
>
> They *aren't fighting* a fire *today*. *They're training*.

2 **Complete the text with the verbs in brackets. Use the present simple or continuous.**

My mum is a police officer. She ¹_____ (work) at a police station in Seoul. She ²_____ (drive) a police car every day. From Monday to Friday, she ³_____ (eat) her lunch at work. Police officers in Korea ⁴_____ (work) at the weekend and at night too.

Today, my mum ⁵_____ (do) something different. She ⁶_____ (visit) a primary school and she ⁷_____ (talk) to the children about her job. The children ⁸_____ (ask) questions about her badges and her radio.

3 **Work in pairs. Ask and answer.**

1 What / wear / school / every / day?

2 What / do / at the weekend?

3 What / your teacher / do / right now?

4 Have breakfast / at the moment?

What do you wear at school every day?

I wear jeans and a T-shirt every day.

LESSON 3 Reading

1 Look at the photo. What is the man doing?

2 What is the film *Walking With Giants* about? Listen and read. 🎧 TR: 5

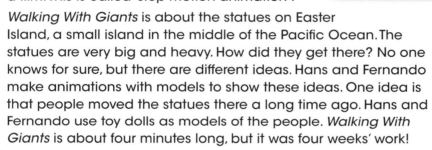

Walking With Giants

Hans Weise is a **film director**. He makes many different kinds of films. He likes making **animations**. There aren't usually any actors in these films. Hans uses **models** instead. He works with a **designer** Fernando Baptista to make models of the people, places and objects. Fernando paints the models and then Hans takes photos of them. After he takes a photo, he moves the models. Then he takes another photo. At the end, he puts all the photos together to make a film. This is called 'stop-motion animation'.

Walking With Giants is about the statues on Easter Island, a small island in the middle of the Pacific Ocean. The statues are very big and heavy. How did they get there? No one knows for sure, but there are different ideas. Hans and Fernando make animations with models to show these ideas. One idea is that people moved the statues there a long time ago. Hans and Fernando use toy dolls as models of the people. *Walking With Giants* is about four minutes long, but it was four weeks' work!

3 Match the words in bold in the text with their meanings.

1 a small copy of something
2 a film people make with drawings or models
3 a person who draws how to make something
4 a person who makes a film

4 Read again. Answer the questions.

1 Who paints the models?
2 What does Hans do before he takes a photo?
3 Why did Hans and Fernando make this film?
4 How long is the film?
5 Would you like to be a film director or a designer? Why?

Grammar

1 **Listen and read.** 🎧 TR: 6

> **Adverbs of frequency**
> We use adverbs of frequency to show how often we do things.
>
> *always*
> *usually*
> *often*
> *sometimes*
> *rarely*
> *never*
>
> We use them <u>before</u> verbs in the present simple, but <u>after</u> the verb *to be*.
> *The designer often <u>makes</u> two or three models.*
> *They <u>are</u> usually difficult to paint.*

2 **Put the adverbs of frequency in Hans Weise's description.**

1 I use toys for people and animals. (sometimes)

2 I put the camera on a table. (always) I hold it in my hand, because it can move. (never)

3 I take a picture of the models, move them a bit and then take another picture. (usually)

4 I take five pictures for each one second of film. (usually) Then I put the pictures on my computer.

5 I have hundreds of pictures. (often) I make the animation with a computer program.

6 It's easy to make animated films, but they are very long. (rarely)

3 **Work in groups. Say true or false sentences about your day. Can your partners guess?**

I always get up before seven o'clock.

That's true.

False!

Moai statues on Easter Island, Chile

Different jobs

I'm in the field.
I'm cutting fields of wheat.
I love my job, I work outside,
I grow the food we eat.

Chorus
Different jobs for different people.
What's my job? Can you guess?

I'm on the plane.
I'm flying through the sky.
I love my job, I travel a lot
To Paris and Mumbai.
Chorus

I'm in the café.
I'm carrying food around.
I love my job, I meet new people
From many different towns.
Chorus

I'm in the class.
I'm teaching maths today.
I love my job, the children learn
And I learn a lot from them!
Chorus

VALUE **Be curious.**
Workbook, Lesson 6

Listen and sing. 🎧 TR: 8 and 9

Sing and act. 🎧 TR: 10

1 Read the interview. What is Kobie's job?

An interview with
Kobie Boykins

Where do you work, Kobie?

I work at NASA in California. NASA is the USA's space agency.

What's your job?

I'm an engineer. I make robots.

Where do your robots go?

They go into space and to other planets, like Mars.

Do you like your job?

Yes, I do. I love it! It's amazing to think that *my* robots are travelling in space at the moment.

What is your favourite robot?

My first robot, called the Sojourner Rover. It was the first robot to go to Mars. It had three cameras on it for taking photos.

What are you working on at the moment?

I'm making a new robot for the next trip to Mars. It has 23 cameras and an arm to pick things up.

2 Read. Then look at the interview again and answer the questions.

When we do an **interview**, we usually follow these steps:

- First, we think about the information we want to know.
- Then, we write some questions.
- Finally, we ask the questions and write the answers.

Which questions are about

1 Kobie's job?
2 how Kobie feels?
3 what Kobie is doing at the moment?
4 Kobie's favourite things?

3 Writing skill Interview questions

a Write three questions for an interview about someone's school.

1 Where / go / school?

_____

2 What / favourite / subject?

_____

3 What / learn / about / at the moment?

_____

b Work in pairs. Ask and answer the questions.

4 Interview someone in your family about his/her job. First, write your questions.

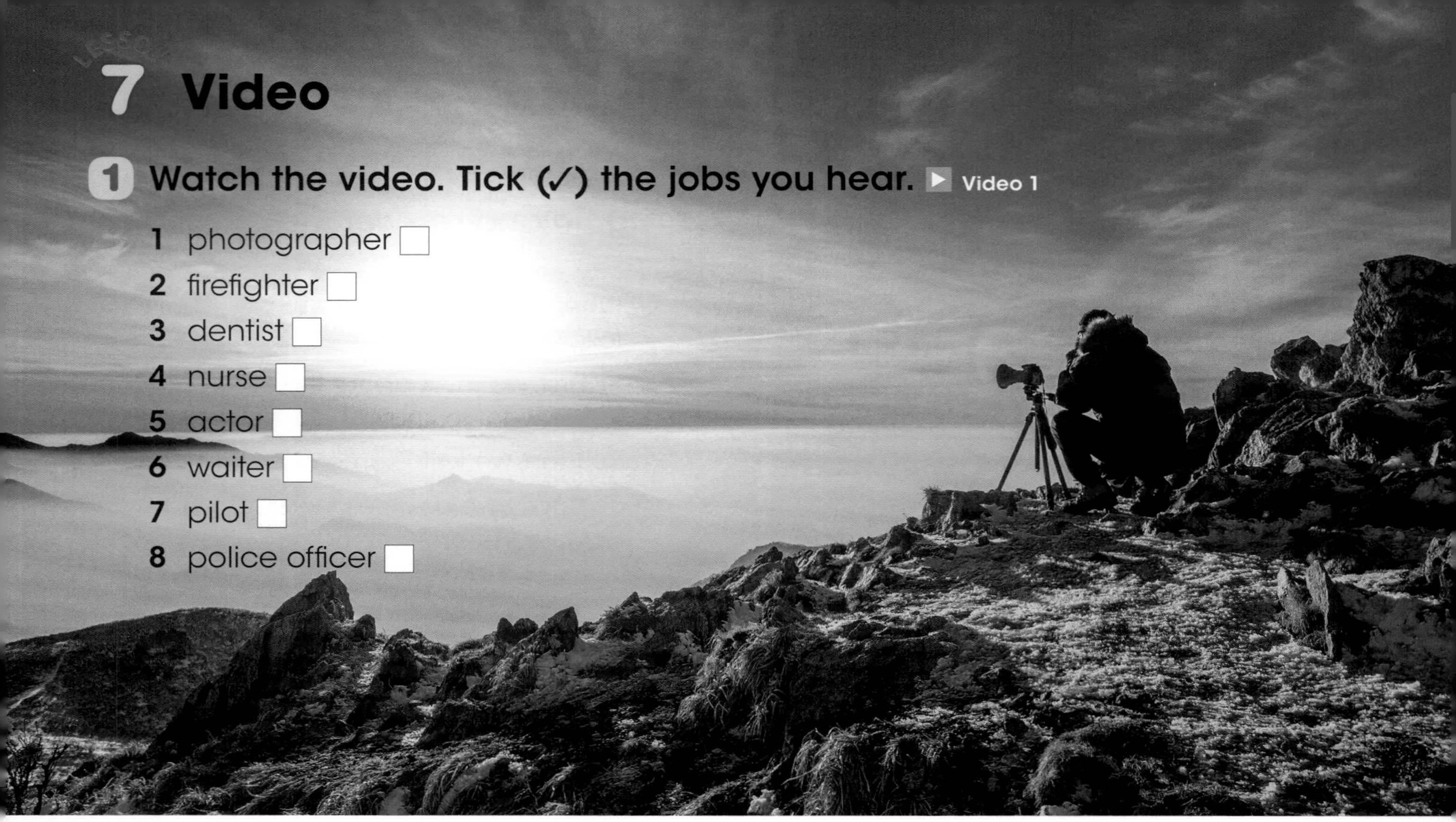

7 Video

1 Watch the video. Tick (✓) the jobs you hear. ▶ Video 1

1 photographer ☐
2 firefighter ☐
3 dentist ☐
4 nurse ☐
5 actor ☐
6 waiter ☐
7 pilot ☐
8 police officer ☐

2 Watch the video again. Match the children with two things that they talk about. ▶ Video 1

1 AJ [C] ☐   2 Rhiane ☐ ☐   3 Lara ☐ ☐

A working in a team
B taking photos of trees
C taking things to villages
D protecting people and forests
E flying over forests
F swimming in the sea

3 Read and write T (true) or F (false).

1 AJ's uncle works in Alaska.
2 There are many forests where AJ's uncle works.
3 Rhiane wants to be a dentist.
4 Rhiane wants to travel when she is older.
5 Lara's dad and grandpa were firefighters.
6 Lara thinks a firefighter has a difficult job.

4 Work in pairs. Discuss the questions.

1 Which of the jobs mentioned in the video do you want to do? Why?
2 Talk about a job someone in your family does.
3 How can you choose the best job for you? What do you have to think about?

Move to the music!

Ice Music Festival in Geilo, Norway

Look at the photo. Answer the questions.

1 What is the woman doing?
2 What is the harp made of?
3 What is she wearing? Why?
4 What musical instruments can you play?

17

cello

classical music

concert

dancer

drums

flute

keyboard

pop music

singer

violin

Complete the text with the words from Exercise 1.

Orchestras are groups of musicians. They give ¹_____ in theatres. They usually play ²_____ music, but they sometimes play ³_____ music too. The musicians play different instruments like the ⁴ **v**_____, the ⁵ **c**_____, the ⁶ **f**_____ or the ⁷ **d**_____. But they don't usually play electric instruments like the ⁸_____. A ⁹_____ sometimes sings a song, but there aren't any ¹⁰_____**s**.

3 Listen to the presentation about the Recycled Orchestra of Cateura. Circle the correct answer. 🎧 TR: 12

1 The orchestra is from *Paraguay / Colombia* in South America.

2 Favio Chavez started the orchestra in *2006 / 2012*.

3 They made instruments from old *cars / tins*.

4 There were music classes every *day / week*.

5 They played their first concert in a different country in *2012 / 2020*.

6 They played in *Brazil / Mexico*.

1 Read and listen. 🎧 TR: 13

> **Past simple: *be***
> *It was their first concert.*
> *It wasn't easy.*
> *Were the instruments expensive?*
> *Yes, they were. / No, they weren't.*
> **Past simple: regular verbs**
> *In 2012, they visited Brazil.*
> *The children didn't play instruments then.*
> *Did you guess? Yes, I did. / No, I didn't.*

2 Complete the text with these verbs. Use the past simple.

> clap   be (x2)   play   love
> watch   visit

This month, we ¹_____ many concerts with an American rock band called Metallica. More than 35,000 people ²_____ us at the first concert. We ³_____ very nervous. But the audience ⁴_____ the concert and they ⁵_____ a lot. We ⁶_____ six different countries in South America. It ⁷_____ an amazing experience!

3 Make sentences in the past simple.

1 Children / not clean / their instruments

2 Favio Chavez / not be / a farmer

3 They / use / paint tins to make instruments

4 It / not be / easy to make the instruments

5 In 2014 / the orchestra / not visit / Europe

4 Think of three things you did yesterday. Ask your partner.

> Did you walk to school yesterday?
> No, I didn't.

Reading

1 Look at the photo. What are they doing?

2 Listen and read. 🎧 TR: 14

INDIAN
music and dance

My name is Soumik Datta. My brother, Souvid, is a photographer. We live in England, but we were born in India. We wanted to learn more about dance and music in India, and we wanted to make a film. So, in 2015, we visited India and saw more than 100 different musicians.

One group of musicians from Karnataka are famous for their dance called 'the Kunitha'. They wear colourful costumes and many of them play the drums. They sing and jump too. All the men are farmers, but they love dancing.

We filmed their show. It was incredible! The dancers **carried** big drums and they **banged** them loudly. They all **shouted** and they kicked their feet. Then they played their drums quietly and some of the dancers **climbed** onto the drums to make a tower. Then they banged their drums quickly. It was very exciting.

You can watch these dancers playing their drums in one of our programmes. We hope you enjoy it!

3 Read again. What did Soumik and Souvid see? Circle the correct answer.

1 The dancers *carried / kicked* their drums to the field.
2 They *jumped / climbed* high in the air and *banged / kicked* their feet.
3 Then the dancers *banged / kicked* their drums loudly and *shouted / climbed* loudly too.
4 Some dancers *climbed / carried* onto the drums.

4 Read again. Correct the sentences.

1 Soumik's brother is a musician.
2 The dancers are all doctors.
3 They always play their drums loudly.
4 The show was boring.

Dancers in Karnataka, India

Grammar LESSON 4

1 **Listen and read.** 🎧 TR: 15

> **Adverbs of manner**
>
> We use adverbs of manner to describe how we do things. They usually go at the end of a sentence.
>
> *They played quietly.*
>
> *They banged the drums loudly.*
>
> An important irregular adverb is *good* → *well.*
>
> *They played well.*

2 **Complete the text with the adverbs of the words in brackets.**

There are many different kinds of drums. The musicians from Karnataka carry big drums and they play them [1] *loudly* (loud). They play them very [2] _____ (good) too! The Orquesta de Cateura have big drums on the floor. They sometimes play them [3] _____ (slow) and sometimes they play them [4] _____ (quick). Pop groups use drums as well. When they play slow songs, they sometimes play them [5] _____ (quiet). Drummers need to listen [6] _____ (careful) to the rhythm.

3 **Answer the questions about you.**

How do you …
1. eat your breakfast every morning?
2. walk to school?
3. talk to your friends?
4. work in class?
5. do your English homework?

> How do you eat your breakfast every morning?

> I eat it quickly!

LESSON 5 Song

1 **Listen and read. How do you dance?** 🎧 TR: 16

At the dance!

Some people danced slowly.
They moved their arms up and down.
Some people danced quickly.
They hopped and jumped around.

Chorus
But no one danced badly.
We danced! We danced! We danced!

Some people danced sadly.
They looked down at the floor.
Some people danced happily.
They smiled and danced some more.
Chorus

Some people danced carefully.
They all moved in a square.
Some people danced wildly.
They jumped high in the air.
Chorus

Some people danced quietly.
Their moves were very neat.
Some people danced loudly.
They shouted and stamped their feet.
Chorus

2 **Listen and sing.** 🎧 TR: 17 and 18

3 **Listen and act.** 🎧 TR: 19

VALUE **Be yourself.**
Workbook, Lesson 6

Guelaguetza festival,
Oaxaca, Mexico

1 Read the review. Did Nick like the show?

2 Read. Then look at Nick's review again and answer the questions.

> A **review** gives information about an event, e.g. a show, film or a book. It usually:
> - says what the event was.
> - says when the event was.
> - describes the good things and explain why they were good.
> - describes the bad things too.

1 What is the review about?

2 When did Nick see the show?

3 What did he like?

4 What bad things does he write about?

3 Writing skill *because*

a Read. Then look at Nick's review again and complete the sentences.

> We use *because* to explain why we like or don't like something.

1 Nick liked the musical *because* _____.

2 Nick liked the flutes _____ _____.

A review of *Annie*   by Nick

Last night, we went to a theatre in New York to see a musical called *Annie*. It's about the adventures of an 11-year-old girl. She's looking for her parents. Some of the story is sad, but it has a happy ending! There's a lot of singing and dancing.

I loved the musical because the songs were great. The actors were very good singers and they danced very well too! There was a big orchestra and it played loudly. There were flutes, violins, cellos and drums. I liked the flutes because they played beautifully in the slow songs. At the end, I clapped for a long time. I didn't want it to end because I loved it so much!

b Match.

1 I liked the costumes because

2 The drummer was great because

3 I liked the actors because

4 I didn't like the end because

A she played about ten different kinds of drum!

B they were very funny.

C it was very sad.

D they were beautiful colours.

4 Write a review of a show you saw at school or at a theatre.

LESSON 7 Video

1 **Watch the video. Match the countries (1–3) with the instruments (A–C).** ▶ Video 2

1 India ☐   2 Spain ☐   3 Scotland ☐

2 **Watch the video again. Complete the definitions with the words.** ▶ Video 2

> chord   loud   popular   stick   traditional

1 When many people like something, we say it is a _____ thing.

2 A short, thin piece of wood is a _____ .

3 Three or more musical notes played at the same time is a _____ .

4 When people in a place do something for many years, we say it is a _____ thing.

5 The opposite of *quiet* is _____ .

3 **Circle the correct answer.**

1 The sitar is usually *more than / less than* a metre long.

2 People use *a pick / their hands and fingers* to play the tabla.

3 Flamenco is typical in the *south / north* of Spain.

4 Flamenco dancers use their *arms / shoes* to make loud sounds.

5 To play the bagpipes, you *blow into / hit* the pipe.

6 You use your *arms / legs* to play the bagpipes.

4 **Work in pairs. Discuss the questions.**

1 What traditional instruments are there in your country? How do you play them?

2 What instruments do your friends and family play?

3 Which instrument would you like to learn? Why?

Where is your house?

Go straight on.

Turn left (at the end of the road).

Turn right (at the supermarket).

The school is on the right.

1 Listen and complete the dialogue. 🎧 TR: 20

Min: Hi, Leo.

Leo: Hi, Min. Where are you? It's late.

Min: I'm lost! Can you help me?

Leo: OK. Where are you now?

Min: I'm on Green Street, near High Street.

Leo: OK. Go straight on down Green Street and [1]_____ at the bookshop.

Min: And then?

Leo: Then [2]_____ and my house is [3]_____. It's number 26.

Min: OK. Thanks, Leo. See you soon.

Leo: Yes. See you soon.

2 Listen, check and repeat. 🎧 TR: 21

3 Read the dialogue again and look at the map. What colour is Leo's house?

HIGH STREET

MIN IS HERE

GREEN STREET

SUPERMARKET

BOOKS

JAMES STREET

CINEMA

SPORTS CENTRE

4 Play a game. Think of a place in your school. In pairs, give directions to your partner. Can your partner find the place?

Go out of the classroom. Turn left. Then go straight on. At the end, turn right ... Where are you?

At the café!

Redwood forests

You're going to watch wildlife photographer, Michael 'Nick' Nichols in action. He's taking photos of the animals and trees in a redwood forest on the west coast of the US. Redwoods are huge trees. Many of the trees are more than 1,500 years old. They're the tallest trees in the world and their trunks can be nine metres thick! They can grow to more than 100 metres tall so it's difficult to take photos of them. Nick needs to find some special ways to do it.

1 **Read about redwood trees. Answer the questions.**

1 How old are the oldest redwood trees?

2 Why is it difficult to take photos of redwood trees?

2 **Watch the video. Put the sentences in order (1–5).** ▶ Video 3

- ☐ **A** Nick takes some great photos of the owls.
- ☐ **B** Nick sends a camera up the tree.
- ☐ **C** Nick gives the owls food.
- ☐ **D** The photos of the tree go into Nick's computer.
- ☐ **E** Nick puts on a costume.

Scientists studying a very tall redwood tree

3 **PROJECT Work in pairs. Make a size chart.**

Draw a chart to show the size of a redwood tree. Compare it with other trees, animals and things.

4 **Tell the class about your chart.**

A redwood tree is 100 metres tall. It's taller than the Statue of Liberty in New York, but it's shorter than the Eiffel Tower in Paris.

Review 1: Units 1–2

1 **Complete the text with these words. There are three words you don't need.**

> actor   carry   climb   concerts   dancer   dentist   drums   pilot

When I'm older, I want to learn how to fly a plane. Maybe I can be a ¹_____ one day. I love music too. I like going to ²_____ at my school. I go to dance classes, but I don't want to be a ³_____ . I always ⁴_____ a camera with me. My sister plays the ⁵_____ and I like taking photos of her. So maybe I can be a photographer. I don't need to decide now!

2 **Choose the best title for the text in Exercise 1.**

The right job for me ☐   My sister's hobby ☐   How to fly a plane ☐

3 **Write sentences about you.**

> always   usually   often   sometimes   rarely   never

1 On my birthday, _____ .
2 At school, _____ .
3 _____ in the summer.
4 At the weekend, _____ .
5 When I'm happy/bored, _____ .

4 **Make sentences and questions. Use the past simple.**

1 she / play / the violin / at the school concert
2 they / not visit / London / yesterday
3 you / climb / up the mountain?
4 we / carry / the drums / onto the stage
5 be / keyboard / expensive?

5 **Complete the sentences with the adverbs of the words in brackets.**

1 The woman played the piano _____ . (quiet)
2 The audience clapped _____ . (loud)
3 The girl danced very _____ . (good)
4 He didn't walk to the concert _____ . (quick)
5 They played their instruments _____ . (careful)

Let's celebrate!

Mercantia, a street art festival in Certaldo, Italy

Look at the photo. Answer the questions.

1 What are the people looking at?

2 What other things do you think they can see in this festival?

3 What celebrations do you have in your area?

29

1 Words

1 Listen and repeat. 🎧 TR: 22

eat traditional food

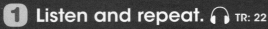
give presents

make special food

play party games

put up decorations

see a parade

throw streamers

wear a costume

2 Answer the questions.

1 Which of these things do you do for / at a party?

2 Which of these things do you do at a street festival?

3 Which do you do at both?

3 Listen to the presentation about a harvest festival in South Korea. Circle the correct answer. 🎧 TR: 23

1 Do people usually celebrate the harvest at the end of autumn? *Yes, they do. / No, they don't.*

2 Did people put up decorations for Chuseok? *Yes, they did. / No, they didn't.*

3 Did they give presents? *Yes, they did. / No, they didn't.*

4 Did people throw streamers in the parade? *Yes, they did. / No, they didn't.*

5 Did people wear traditional costumes? *Yes, they did. / No, they didn't.*

1 **Listen and read.** 🎧 TR: 24

> **Past simple: irregular verbs**
> *We **ate** traditional food.*
> *They **didn't eat** pizza.*
> ***Did** people **wear** costumes?*
> *Yes, they **did**. / No, they **didn't**.*
>
> | | | |
> |---|---|---|
> | eat – ate | have – had | see – saw |
> | give – gave | make – made | throw – threw |
> | go – went | put – put | wear – wore |

2 **Complete the text with the verbs in brackets. Use the past simple.**

Last weekend, I was at the Apple Harvest Festival, here in Pennsylvania, US. We ¹_____ (make) twenty apple pies before the festival. We ²_____ (go) to the festival early and I ³_____ (put up) decorations with my family. We ⁴_____ (eat) many different kinds of food. My favourite was the toffee apples! The festival is really big. I ⁵_____ (not / see) all of it. But I ⁶_____ (see) lots of my friends there and we ⁷_____ (dance) to the music together.

3 **Make questions to ask your friend about a festival.**

> dance   eat   give   make   play   put up
> see   throw   wear

4 **Ask your questions from Exercise 3.**

> Did you dance at your party?

> No, I didn't. But I listened to the music.

Parade to celebrate Chuseok in Seoul, South Korea with girls and women wearing traditional 'hanbok' dresses

1 Look at the photo of a festival in Italy. Which of the chocolates would you like to try?

2 Listen and read. 🎧 TR: 25

Wonderful food festivals in Italy

Mica

Where did you go?
We went to Florence in May. We went to the Ice Cream Festival!

What did you do?
The festival was in a big square on a hill. We **bought** a ticket and walked around the festival. We ate many different flavours of ice cream. One was milk, honey and rice flavour, but my favourite was orange, lemon and mint. People **chose** their favourite ice cream flavour to see who was the best ice cream maker. At the end of the festival, we **took** photos with the ice cream makers!

Anna

Where did you go?
We went to Perugia in October. We went to the Chocolate Festival!

What did you do?
On the first day, we watched people on the street. They made sculptures from huge pieces of chocolate. They were beautiful, and we ate some of the chocolate too! At the Chocolate Museum, we **learnt** about how people make chocolate. The next day, we **drank** some delicious hot chocolate.

3 Read again. Write T (true) or F (false).

1 The Ice Cream Festival is in October. ▪
2 Mica liked the milk, honey and rice flavour more than the orange, lemon and mint flavour. ▪
3 There was a competition for the best ice cream. ▪
4 The Chocolate Festival is in Perugia. ▪
5 At the museum, Anna learnt how to make sculptures. ▪
6 Anna didn't like the hot chocolate. ▪

4 Find the past simple of these verbs in the text.

1 buy
2 choose
3 drink
4 learn
5 take

1 Listen and read. 🎧 TR: 26

> **Past simple: *Wh-* questions**
> *Where did you go?*
> *We went to Florence.*
> *What did you eat?*
> *We ate ice cream.*
> **Past simple: *Wh-* questions with *be***
> *What was your favourite flavour?*
> *Strawberry was my favourite!*

2 Put the questions in order. Look at the text on page 32 again and write the answers.

1 did / where / go / Mica

_____?

_____

2 did / buy / he / what

_____?

_____

3 did / Perugia / Anna / when / go / to

_____?

_____

4 make / what / people / from chocolate pieces / did

_____?

_____

5 eat / Anna / did / what

_____?

_____

3 Think about a festival or a celebration you went to. Ask and answer questions.

> What ...?   Where ...?   When ...?   Why ...?

> be   drink   eat   go   make   see   wear

1 Listen and read. Do you have street parties?
What other celebrations do you have with your neighbours? 🎧 TR: 27

Our Street Party

Chorus
Today was our street party.
It was a lot of fun.
We all came together.
There was something for everyone.

What did you make?
What did you see?
Tell us all about it, please!

We made decorations. We made costumes.
We saw dance shows. We saw races.
We all came together.
There was something for everyone.

Chorus

What did you drink?
What did you eat?
Tell us all about it, please!

We drank milkshakes. We drank fruit juice.
We ate pancakes. We ate pizza.
We all worked together.
And there was something for everyone.

Chorus

2 Listen and sing. 🎧 TR: 28 and 29

3 Sing and act. 🎧 TR: 30

VALUE **Be a good neighbour.**
Workbook, Lesson 6

1 Read Uma's email. Why was she tired?

To: Toby

From: Uma

Subject: A wedding!

Hi Toby,

How are you? My weekend was fun! Yesterday, it was my aunt's wedding party.

First of all, I went with my mum to help with the preparations. We made big circles of flowers for people to wear around their necks and in their hair. Later, we watched the marriage ceremony. My aunt and uncle drank a special drink. It was milk with banana. After the ceremony, we went home to change our clothes. I wore a blue and gold dress. Then, we went back to the wedding. Everyone danced and sang. At the end, we all threw flower petals on my aunt and uncle! It was beautiful and everyone was very happy.

I went home to bed at 11 o'clock. I was very tired!

See you soon!

Uma

2 Read. Then look at Uma's email again and answer the questions.

In an **email** describing an event, we:
- write a subject in the subject line.
- start with a greeting.
- describe what happened.
- say goodbye at the end.

1 What is the subject of her email?

2 How does she say hello and goodbye?

3 What verbs does she use to describe the events?

3 **Writing skill** Time connectors

a **Read and answer the question.**

We use these time connectors to explain when things happened.

> first of all   then
> after (the ceremony)   at the end

Do they go at the beginning or the end of a sentence?

b **Complete Toby's email to Uma with time connectors.**

Hi Uma,

That sounds like a great wedding. I had a great Saturday too.

¹_____ , I had a swimming competition, and I came second. ²_____ , we had lunch in my favourite café. ³_____ lunch, my cousins visited us and we went to a summer street party. We watched the school band. They were great! ⁴_____ , we said goodbye to our cousins and went home.

See you soon.

Toby

4 Write an email to a friend about a celebration you went to.

festivals (A–C). ▶ Video 4

1 Japan ☐   **2** the US ☐   **3** Mexico ☐

2 **Watch the video again. Match the children with two things they talk about.** ▶ Video 4

1 Yurara ☐C☐   **2** AJ ☐☐   **3** Marlen ☐☐

A music and dance   **D** taking photos

B a festival in August   **E** sculptures made of sand

C fireworks   **F** colourful costumes

3 **Answer the questions.**

1 Who did Yurara go to the Fireworks festival with?

2 What does she say about the food they had?

3 In which month is the Sandsations festival?

4 What do the artists use to make the sculptures?

5 How long does the Guelaguetza festival last?

6 What does the festival celebrate?

4 **Work in pairs. Discuss the questions.**

1 What different festivals are there in your country? Which is your favourite?

2 What festivals and celebrations from other countries do you know about?

3 Which would you like to go to most? Why?

Students at a school in Seoul, South Korea

Look at the photo. Answer the questions.

1 What sport are they doing?

2 Why do you think they enjoy it?

3 Would you like to do this sport?

37

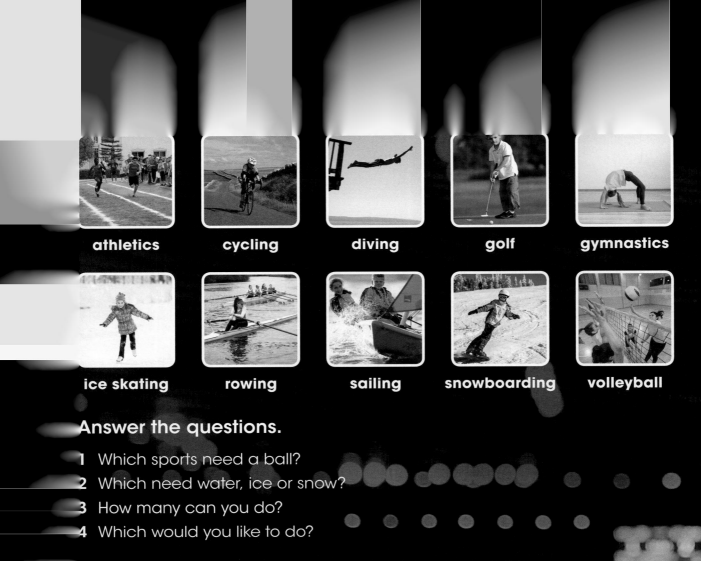

athletics   **cycling**   **diving**   **golf**   **gymnastics**

ice skating   **rowing**   **sailing**   **snowboarding**   **volleyball**

Answer the questions.

1 Which sports need a ball?
2 Which need water, ice or snow?
3 How many can you do?
4 Which would you like to do?

Listen to the conversation about a Paralympic sport for people who can't see well. Complete the information. 🎧 TR: 32

GOALBALL

History: Two men invented the game in ¹_____ .

Rules: There are ²_____ players in each team.

Teams take turns to ³_____ the ball.

All players wear masks to cover their ⁴_____ .

They can't see the ball, but they can ⁵_____ it.

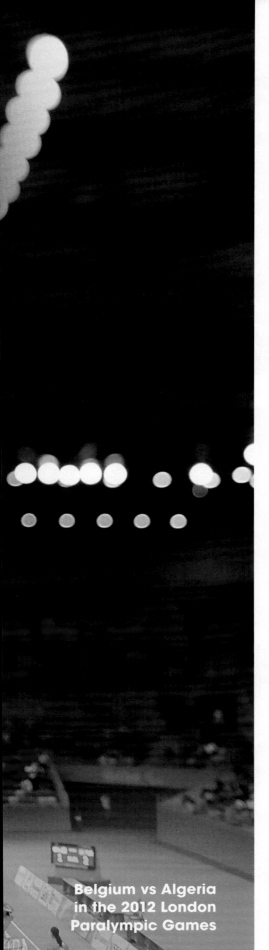

Belgium vs Algeria in the 2012 London Paralympic Games

Grammar

1 **Listen and read.** 🎧 TR: 33

> ***Can* and *could***
>
> **Present**
>
> They **can** hear the ball.
>
> They **can't** see the ball.
>
> **Past**
>
> They **could** see, but not very well.
>
> They **couldn't** play any sports.

2 **Complete the text with *can*, *can't*, *could* or *couldn't*.**

Some sports, like golf, volleyball and basketball are difficult for blind people to play. But there are many sports they ¹_____ play. They ²_____ win medals too. Jen Armbruster is an American goalball player. When she was a teenager, Jen was in the school basketball team. She ³_____ play really well. But at the age of 14, she began to have eye problems and soon she ⁴_____ see at all. Then she ⁵_____ play basketball any more. But there was a sport she ⁶_____ play: goalball! She joined the Olympic team when she was 16. In 2008, she won a gold medal.

3 **What could you do at the age of five? Make two sentences.**

> talk in ...   read   walk   ride a bike   play basketball

I could read, but I couldn't talk in English.

4 **Work in pairs. Ask and answer questions about your sentences from Exercise 3.**

Could you play basketball?

No, I couldn't. But I could ride a bike.

3 Reading

1 Look at the photo. Why is there only one swimmer?

2 Listen and read. 🎧 TR: 34

The Olympic dream!

Eric Moussambani was a star at the Olympics in Sydney in 2000. The swimmer from Equatorial Guinea didn't win a medal, but the crowd loved him.

Eric only started swimming in January 2000. He was 21 years old. He practised in a small swimming pool in a hotel. When he saw the Olympic pool in Sydney, he was **surprised**. It was huge! It was 50 metres long. He couldn't see the other end of it! The pool at home was only 12 metres long.

In Eric's race, there were two other swimmers. But they both jumped in the pool too early and the referee stopped the race. When the race started again, Eric was the only swimmer and he was **nervous**. Everyone watched him. He started to swim very quickly, but soon he felt very **tired**. The crowd cheered "Eric! Eric!" This helped him to finish. After the race, Eric was a hero. His time was very slow, but it didn't matter. People thought he was very **brave**.

In 2016, Eric went to the Olympics in Rio de Janeiro, Brazil. He didn't swim for Equatorial Guinea. He was the team's coach!

3 Answer the questions.

1 When did Eric start swimming?
2 Where were the Olympic Games in 2000?
3 How long was the pool in the hotel?
4 How did Eric feel before the race?
5 What did the crowd shout?
6 Did Eric finish the race?

4 Work in pairs. What do these adjectives mean? Then answer the questions.

brave   nervous   surprised   tired

1 Talk about a person who did something brave.
2 What makes you feel nervous?
3 When was the last time you were surprised?
4 When do you feel tired?

Eric Moussambani swims alone in the 2000 Olympic Games

1 **Listen and read.** 🎧 TR: 35

> **Object pronouns**
>
> *Can you help me?*   *Did you see us?*
>
> *Can I watch the race with you?*   *He waved to them.*
>
> *Everyone watched him.*
>
> *He threw the ball back to her.*
>
> *He couldn't see the other end of it.*

2 **Complete the text with object pronouns.**

Olympic and Paralympic stories

- In 1956, a Russian rower, Viktor Ivanov, dropped his silver medal in the lake. A 13-year-old student found [1]_____ in the water and returned it to [2]_____ .

- In 1960, Abebe Bikila won the marathon. His new running shoes didn't fit very well, so he ran without [3]_____ !

- Wilma Rudolph won two gold medals in 1960. She ran in the 100 metres and 200 metres. People called [4]_____ 'the tornado'.

- Derek Redmond fell in a race in 1992. His father helped [5]_____ to finish [6]_____ .

3 **Complete the questions with object pronouns. Then answer them.**

1 What sports do you do? Why do you like doing _____?

2 Do you do sports alone, or do other people play with _____?

3 Which sport do you like watching on TV? Do you play _____ with your friends too?

4 Who is your favourite sportsman? Why do you like _____?

5 Who is your favourite sportswoman? Why do you like _____?

5 Song

1 Listen and read. What do you like about doing sport? 🎧 TR: 36

Running for fun

When I was young,
I didn't like sport.
I wasn't good at it.
"It's boring," I thought.

But when I was older,
I went out in the sun.
I started to row.
And I started to run.
… And it was fun!
It didn't matter if I lost or won.
I had fun with my friends.
Yes, I had fun with them!

I didn't like teams.
I didn't like to race.
I wasn't good at it,
Always in last place.

But when I was older,
I went out in the sun.
I started to cycle.
And I started to jump.
… And it was fun!
It didn't matter if I lost or won.
I had fun with my friends.
Yes, I had fun with them!

2 Listen and sing. 🎧 TR: 37 and 38

3 Sing and act. 🎧 TR: 39

VALUE Have fun doing sport.
Workbook, Lesson 6

1 **What do you know about these people? Read and find out.**

2 **Read. Then look at the factfiles again and answer the questions.**

> A **factfile** for a person shows you some important information about them. This can include:
> - their name and what they do
> - personal information, e.g. their birthday and birth place
> - facts about things they did in the past.

1 What do these two people do?

2 When were they born?

3 What did they do when they were young?

3 **Writing skill** Using *when*

a **Find *when* in the factfiles. What punctuation do we use after the *when* clause?**

b **Match to make sentences about the Australian cyclist, Anna Meares.**

1 When she was young, …

2 When she was 11, …

3 When she was 20, …

4 When she was 28, …

A she won her second Olympic gold medal.

B she started cycling.

C she won her first Olympic gold medal.

D she didn't cycle. She did karate and she played tennis.

4 **Write a factfile about a famous sportsperson.**

Name:
Usain Bolt

Sport:
Athletics

Date of birth:
21st August, 1986

Place of birth:
Jamaica

Nickname:
Lightning Bolt

* When he was young, he played cricket and football.
* When he was 12, he was the fastest runner in his school at 100 metres.
* When he was 21, he broke the world record for 100 metres.
* Five days before his 22nd birthday, he won his first Olympic gold medal.

Name:
Annika Sörenstam

Sport:
Golf

Date of birth:
9th October, 1970

Place of birth:
Sweden

Nickname:
Miss 59

* When she was young, she liked skiing, tennis and football.
* When she was 12, her parents bought her some golf clubs.
* When she was 16, she played in the Swedish team.
* When she was 24, she won her first big tournament.

Video

1 **Watch the video. Which famous sportspeople do the children talk about?** ▶ Video 5

2 **Watch the video again. Write B (Bruce Lee), P (Pelé) or W (Wilma Rudolph).** ▶ Video 5

1 _____ could run fast with a football.
2 _____ could run 100 metres in 11 seconds.
3 _____ could do kung fu.
4 _____ couldn't walk when they were young.
5 _____ could score goals with their head.

3 **Read and write T (true) or F (false).**

1 Bruce Lee was an actor.
2 Bruce Lee died when he was 73.
3 Pelé's real name wasn't *Pelé*.
4 Pelé won the World Cup three times with Brazil.
5 Wilma Rudolph was called 'the tornado' because she was fast.
6 Wilma Rudolph won medals in three Olympic Games.

4 **Work in pairs. Discuss the questions.**

1 Which person from the video would you like to know more about, and what?
2 Who were some important sportspeople from your country? Why were they famous?
3 Which sport would you like to do well? Why?

1 Play the game in small groups. Follow the instructions.

Start

What did you do last summer?

What did you buy on Saturday?

Move forward two spaces!

What did you eat for lunch yesterday?

When did you last buy a book?

What sports could you do when you were six?

Where was your first home?

When was the last time you celebrated something?

What did you wear on Sunday?

What time did you have breakfast this morning?

Move forward three spaces!

What did you drink at lunchtime?

What was the last present you got?

Miss a turn!

When did you last cycle?

When did you last swim?

What did you watch on TV at the weekend?

What sport did you do this week?

Where did you go at the weekend?

Who did you talk to first today?

How did you get to school on Monday?

Move forward two spaces!

What music did you listen to yesterday?

What did you learn at school today?

What did you eat for dinner yesterday?

Finish

Instructions

Take turns to throw a coin.
- One side = move forward two spaces
- Other side = move forward one space

You must answer each question with a sentence. You must answer in 15 seconds. If you don't answer correctly, you go back one space. The first player to the FINISH wins!

The tightrope across
Niagara Falls

There was once a famous tightrope walker named Charles Blondin. He lived about 150 years ago. Blondin could do many amazing things on a tightrope: he could stand on one leg; he could sit on a chair; he could stop and make something to eat; he could even walk with his eyes closed.

Blondin came from France, but he did many famous tightrope walks across the Niagara Falls, between Canada and the USA – a distance of 340 metres, and 50 metres above the water. People said that it was impossible and that he could never do it. But Blondin did it, not just once but many times. And each time a crowd waited on the other side of the water to watch him. And each time they cheered loudly when he arrived.

There are many stories about Blondin. People say that one time, he crossed the Falls pushing a wheelbarrow with potatoes in it. The crowd watched. They couldn't believe their eyes. 'Ooh!' and 'Aaah!' they shouted as he walked carefully to the other side. When he arrived, they cheered more loudly than ever.

He put down the wheelbarrow and looked at the crowd.

'So, do you think I can walk back across the Falls with the wheelbarrow?' he asked them.

'Yes, you can!' they all shouted.

'And do you think I can walk back with a man in the wheelbarrow too?' he asked.

'Yes!' they shouted again. 'You are the greatest tightrope walker in the world. You can do anything.'

'OK,' said Blondin. He waited for a moment. 'Then who wants to climb into the wheelbarrow?' he asked. He looked at the people, but they were all very quiet.

Glossary

tightrope A long rope, high above the ground. Acrobats walk along it.

wheelbarrow It has one wheel and two handles. People use it for carrying things.

cheer to shout because you like something

crowd a big group of people

Jay Cochrane
walks on a
tightrope across
the Niagara Falls.

1 Look at the acrobat in the photo. What is he doing? What kind of person do you think he is?

2 Listen and read. Did Blondin walk across Niagara Falls? 🎧 TR: 40

3 Read again and answer the questions.

1 What four amazing things could Blondin do on a tightrope?

2 How long was the tightrope across the Niagara Falls?

3 What did Blondin put in the wheelbarrow before he crossed the Niagara Falls?

4 Did the crowd think that Blondin could push a person across the Niagara Falls?

5 Who wanted to climb into the wheelbarrow?

4 Complete the sentences. Use one, two or three words in each gap.

1 No one thought that Blondin _____ across the Niagara Falls.

2 But Blondin walked across the Falls _____ than once.

3 _____ cheered every time he did it.

4 In one story, _____ potatoes in Blondin's wheelbarrow.

5 No one in the crowd _____ to climb into the wheelbarrow.

5 Work in pairs. Discuss the questions.

1 Who thought Blondin could cross the Falls with a person in the wheelbarrow?

2 Why did no one want to climb into the wheelbarrow?

3 Do you think it is a good story? Why? / Why not?

1 Complete.

costume   decorations   parade   party games   presents

1 Can you help me to put up the _____?
2 Are you going to wear a _____ for this party?
3 There are lots of people playing music in the _____ this year.
4 Do you give _____ to people at this festival?
5 What _____ do children your age play?

2 Look and write.

_____   _____   _____   _____   _____

3 Complete the questions with these words. Then answer them in pairs.

who   where   did   was   what

1 _____ did you go yesterday?
2 _____ did you go with?
3 _____ did you eat?

4 _____ the weather good?
5 _____ you have a good time?

4 Make sentences using *can*, *can't*, *could* or *couldn't*.

	ice skate	speak French	run quickly	ride a bike
7 years old	✗	✗	✓	✗
Now	✓	✓	✗	✓

When I was seven years old, I couldn't ice skate. Now, I can ice skate.

5 Complete the conversation with object pronouns.

A: Felix, there's a competition at the swimming pool this afternoon. I'm going to see ¹_____ with Edu. Why don't you come with ²_____ ?

B: I'm not sure. My mum is helping ³_____ with my homework.

A: You can ask ⁴_____ to help ⁵_____ do ⁶_____ now. Oh, and my cousins are coming too. I want you to meet ⁷_____ .

B: OK, great! See ⁸_____ there.

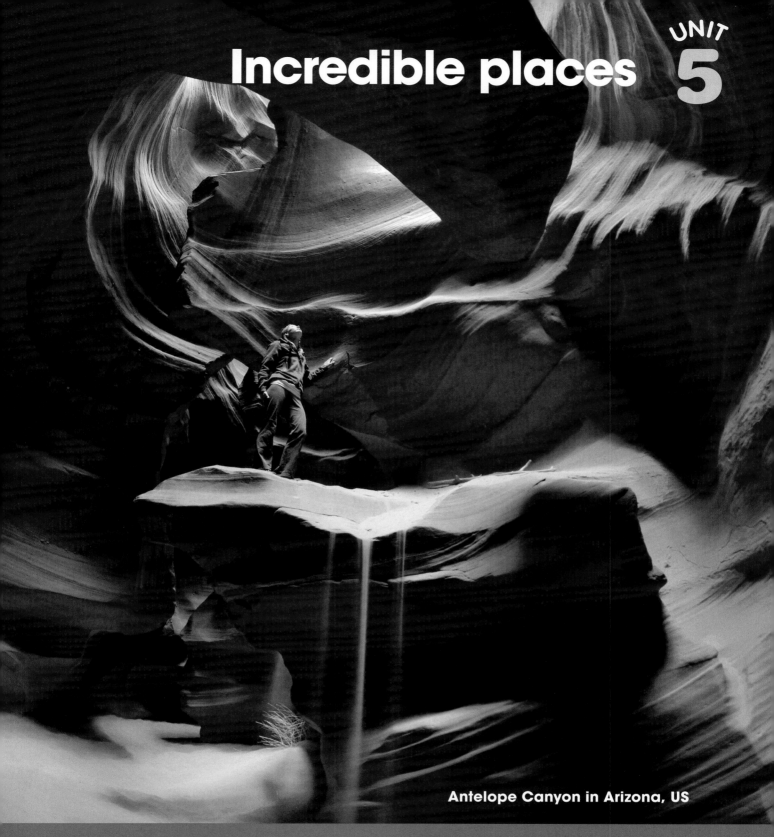

Incredible places

Antelope Canyon in Arizona, US

Look at the photo. Answer the questions.

1 How can you describe this place?

2 What could you do here?

3 Would you like to visit this place? Why? / Why not?

4 What kind of places do you like to visit?

49

1 Words

1 Listen and repeat. 🎧 TR: 41

 **bridge**

 **castle**

 **cave**

 **island**

 **jungle**

 **desert**

 **plant**

 **pyramid**

 **rock**

 **wave**

2 Complete the text with words from the box.

> castle   island   jungle   plants   rock   waves

Last month, my family and I visited Borneo, an
¹_____ in Southeast Asia. On the first day, we
went into the ²_____ to see all the animals
and ³_____ there! We saw a proboscis
monkey sitting on a ⁴_____ . This monkey
had a really big nose! The next day, we went to the
beach. My brother and I made a ⁵_____ in
the sand. I surfed the big ⁶_____ , too!

3 Listen to a conversation about Yucatan in Mexico. Circle the correct answer. 🎧 TR: 42

1 Harry's holiday *started / finished* on Saturday.

2 Harry swam with *sharks / sea turtles*.

3 In the jungles of Yucatán there are more than 1,400 types of *animals / plants*.

4 The pyramids are *near the beach / in the jungle*.

5 The Kukulkan Pyramid is sometimes called '*The Castle*' / '*The Square*'.

6 Harry *went / didn't go* inside the Kukulkan Pyramid.

Grammar

1 **Listen and read.** 🎧 TR: 43

> **Comparatives and superlatives**
>
> tall · *The pyramid is taller than the trees.*
>
> big · *The USA is bigger than Mexico.*
>
> large · *The largest building is the Kukulkan Pyramid.*
>
> busy · *It's the busiest place in the city.*
>
> good > **better** > **the best**
>
> bad > **worse** > **the worst**
>
> far > **further** > **the furthest**

2 **Compare these places. Use comparatives.**

- lake / sea
- desert / jungle
- town / village
- castle / school

A sea is usually larger than a lake.

3 **Complete the facts with the superlative form of the adjectives in brackets.**

1 In 2018, divers in the Yucatán discovered the _____ (long) underwater cave. It's 347 kilometres long!

2 The _____ (old) paintings in the world are in a cave in northern Spain. They are 40,800 years old!

3 The Atacama Desert in Chile is the _____ (dry) desert in the world.

4 The _____ (hot) ocean in the world is the Indian Ocean.

5 Many people think the _____ (good) waves for surfing are in Australia.

4 **Write four questions using comparatives and superlatives. Ask and answer with a partner.**

- Animals
- Places
- Sports
- Music

> What's bigger, an elephant or a rhino?

> An elephant is bigger than a rhino.

Kukulkan Pyramid in Yucatán, Mexico

Reading

1 Look at the photo. Name three things you see.

2 Listen and read. 🎧 TR: 44

The desert sands!

Dubai is the largest and most **important** city in the United Arab Emirates. Dubai is by the sea, but all the land around it is desert. Many people want to work and live there. The most **popular** place to live is by the beach. It is much cooler there. But there isn't much space to live by the beach any more. In 2001, people started to build the Jumeirah islands on the water. They used rocks and sand to make them. They look like palm trees!

Outside Dubai, there are huge hills of sand called 'dunes'. There are thousands of kilometres of them. There is an **exciting** sport you can do on them: sandboarding! This is the same as snowboarding, but it's on sand instead of snow! It's great fun but you need to be careful too – it is **dangerous** to be in the hot sun for a long time. Drive up to the top of the dunes, then sandboard down. The worst part is that you have to walk back up afterwards!

3 Read again. Write T (true) or F (false).

1 There are other cities in the United Arab Emirates that are bigger than Dubai.

2 In Dubai, people usually want to live near the beach because it is cooler there.

3 People made the Jumeirah islands.

4 There are dunes inside the city of Dubai.

5 There are thousands of kilometres of snow outside Dubai.

4 What do the adjectives in bold refer to in the text? Complete the sentences.

1 Some sports are _____ if you don't wear a helmet.

2 I hope the film is _____ . I don't want to see a boring film.

3 It is _____ that you wear sun cream in the hot sun.

4 Many people visit the shopping centres in Dubai. They are very _____ places to go.

5 Discuss the questions.

1 Would you like to visit Dubai? Why? / Why not?

2 Can you discover more things about Dubai? Tell your partner about them.

1 Listen and read. 🎧 TR: 45

> **Comparatives and superlatives: long adjectives**
>
> *The homes by the beach are more popular than the homes in the city.*
>
> *Dubai is the most important city in the United Arab Emirates.*

2 Complete the sentences with the comparative or superlative form of the adjectives in brackets.

In 2008, Burj Khalifa became ¹_____ (tall) building in the world. It's in Dubai. It was one of ²_____ (expensive) projects ever. It cost 1.5 billion dollars. It is ³_____ (famous) than other buildings in Dubai. I'd love to go there. It has ⁴_____ (high) restaurant in the world too, on the 122ⁿᵈ floor! Some people say that the view from the top is ⁵_____ (exciting) at night than during the day.

3 Make sentences about these topics. Use the comparative or superlative form of these adjectives.

• Films   • School subjects   • People   • Free-time activities

> dangerous   difficult   exciting   famous   important   interesting   popular

4 Work in pairs. Compare your sentences from Exercise 3. Do you agree?

Maths is the most difficult subject.

I don't agree. I think art is the most difficult subject.

One of the Jumeirah islands in Dubai

1 **Listen and read. Which place would you like to go to?** 🎧 TR: 46

Let's explore!

Chorus
Let's explore! Let's explore!
See the world outside our door.
There's so much to do and see.
So please come along with me!

Let's go down into a cave!
Are you feeling very brave?
There may be a bat or snake.
But we can swim deep in the lake!
Don't be scared, you're with me.
Just come along and you'll see!
Chorus

There's a castle made of stone.
Let's climb up it on our own.
We can see the furthest town,
And the people on the ground.
Climb up, you and me.
Just come along and you'll see!
Chorus

2 **Listen and sing.** 🎧 TR: 47 and 48

3 **Sing and act.** 🎧 TR: 49

VALUE **Explore new places.**
Workbook, Lesson 6

Sequoia trees in California, USA

Writing A travel brochure

1 Read the travel brochure. Would you like to go there? Why? / Why not?

2 Read. Then look at the travel brochure again and do tasks 1–3.

> A **travel brochure**:
> - presents interesting information about a place.
> - uses pictures and exciting descriptions.
> - gives useful information about visiting a place.

1 Find a sentence that gives information about the place.

2 Find a sentence that makes you want to visit the place.

3 Find a sentence with some useful information.

3 **Writing skill** Capital letters

a **Read the information in the box.**

> We use capital letters for:
> - the first word of a sentence
> - names of people, places and things
> - days and months

b **Underline the letters that should be capital letters.**

1 she visited finland in october.

2 let's visit jeanne in london on thursday.

3 the george hotel is the best.

4 grandma wants to go to new york.

4 Think about a special place. Write a travel brochure.

Visit Finland
Stay warm and enjoy the show!

People travel to Lapland, Finland from around the world to see the Northern Lights. It's the most amazing natural show. At Kakslauttanen Resort, you can see the Northern Lights from your own igloo! Lie down in your bed and look through the glass roof. You've got the best view of this brilliant show. And you are warmer and more comfortable than the people standing in the snow!

When to go
- The best time to see the Northern Lights is between September and March.

Transport
- There's a bus to our resort from Ivalo Airport. We also have a bus with a glass roof for large groups!

What to wear
- It's very cold in the winter: between 0°C and -40°C. Don't forget your hat, gloves, boots and a warm coat!

We can't wait to see you!

1 Watch the video. Which country is each place in? ▶ Video 6

1 Italy ☐   **2** Brazil ☐   **3** China ☐

A

B

C

2 Watch the video again. Complete the sentences with the superlative form of these adjectives. ▶ Video 6

> high (x2)   long (x2)   tall

1 The _____ mountain in the Dolomites is called Marmolada.

2 The Amazon is one of the _____ rivers in the world.

3 The _____ rock in the Zhangjiajie Park is more than 1,000 metres.

4 The Glass Bridge is the _____ and _____ bridge in the world.

3 Answer the questions.

1 How high is the Marmolada?

2 What can people do on the lakes?

3 How long is the Amazon river?

4 What do scientists do there?

5 What do the rocks in the Zhangjiajie Park look like?

6 Does the glass skywalk go around a rock, a bridge or a mountain?

4 Work in pairs. Discuss the questions.

1 Which of the places in the video would you like to visit? Why?

2 What's the most popular natural place in your country? Where is it?

3 Why is it popular? What can people do there?

A day out in the Dubai desert

Look at the photo. Answer the questions.

1 What is the boy wearing?

2 Do you like his clothes? Why? / Why not?

3 What do you usually wear at the weekend?

4 What's your favourite item of clothing?

1 Listen and read. 🎧 TR: 50

These children are wearing colourful coats with **pockets**. They look really warm and **comfortable**. A girl is wearing **striped leggings** and another is wearing **spotted** leggings. A boy is wearing **plain** yellow trousers and black **trainers**. All the girls are wearing **sunglasses**. Two of them are wearing **bracelets** too!

2 Complete the sentences with words from Exercise 1.

1 Do you wear _____ or boots when you play football?

2 I usually wear _____ when it's sunny. They protect my eyes.

3 Where are my keys? They're not in my _____.

4 I can move well in these clothes. They are very _____.

5 I don't like striped or spotted clothes. I prefer _____ clothes.

3 Listen to Angela Lan, a young fashion designer. Choose the correct answer. 🎧 TR: 51

1 When she was nine, Angela …

  A wrote a book about fashion.

  B started to make clothes.

  C worked as a fashion model.

2 Angela's favourite trousers …

  A have black and white stripes.

  B are spotted and colourful.

  C are striped and colourful.

3 What's the second item Angela talks about?

  A her sunglasses

  B a pair of trainers

  C a white jacket

4 Angela's favourite coat …

  A has big pockets.

  B is perfect for warm weather.

  C is colourful.

Angela Lan

4 Design your own clothes. Draw a picture of yourself in these clothes. Describe them to a partner.

Autumn-winter 2016 fashion show in Moscow, Russia

1 **Listen and read.** 🎧 TR: 52

> **Possessive pronouns**
>
> *__Whose__ striped shirt is this? It's __mine__.*
>
> | my shoes | *Those shoes are __mine__.* |
> | your hat | *Is this hat __yours__?* |
> | his shirt | *The red shirt is __his__.* |
> | her sunglasses | *The sunglasses on the table are __hers__.* |
> | our towels | *Those towels are __ours__.* |
> | their coats | *Where are Mina and Jane? Are these coats __theirs__?* |

2 **Complete the sentences with possessive pronouns.**

1 You can't use that pen. It's not _____ .

2 _____ coat is this? I really like it.

3 **A:** Are these your sunglasses?

   B: Yes, they're _____ .

4 Where are Jack and Finn? These drinks are _____ .

5 No, those trainers aren't _____ . Her trainers are blue.

3 **In groups, pass a bag around. Each person puts three objects in the bag. Ask and answer questions about each object.**

> Whose pencil case is this? Is it yours, Laura?

> It isn't mine. Pablo, is it yours?

> Yes, it is!

Reading

1 Listen and read. 🎧 TR: 53

Odd Socks Day

We usually wear socks to keep our feet warm. But socks can have a message too!

Who says your socks need to **match**? It was Odd Socks Day on Monday 13th November and we celebrated it at our school last week. We met in the playground at 8.45 before school started. Everyone wore different socks on each foot. It was a lot of fun, but why did we do it?

Well, all week we talked about bullying at school. A bully is a person who **hurts** or **frightens** other people. Older and stronger children sometimes bully the younger, **weaker** children, or children who are different to them. We want to stop bullying at our school. So, on Odd Socks Day, we wear different socks to show everyone that it is good to be different and that all children are important. Everyone needs to feel happy and safe at school.

Let's stop bullying!

2 Match the words in bold in the text with their meanings.

1 less strong
2 to look the same as another thing
3 to make someone feel unhappy
4 to make someone feel scared

3 Read again. Write T (true) or F (false).

1 Odd Socks Day is next week. ☐
2 School started before 8.45. ☐
3 On Odd Socks Day, students wear socks that match. ☐
4 A bully makes other children feel safe. ☐
5 Children sometimes bully other children who are different to them. ☐

4 Discuss the questions.

1 Is Odd Socks Day a good idea? Why? / Why not?

2 What things can you do to help other students feel happy at school?

3 Do you sometimes wear special clothes for a celebration? When?

1 Listen and read. 🎧 TR: 54

> **Infinitive of purpose**
>
> *We usually wear socks **to keep** our feet warm.*
>
> *We wear odd socks **to show** everyone that it is good to be different.*

2 Match to make sentences.

1 We wear hats   **A** to protect our eyes.

2 We wear sunglasses   **B** to keep our hands warm.

3 We use umbrellas   **C** to show that we like a team.

4 We wear football shirts   **D** to keep our heads warm.

5 We wear gloves   **E** to protect us from the rain.

3 What do you use each object for? Discuss.

I use a smartphone to call my parents.

4 Work in pairs. You're on a desert island. Choose four of these objects and explain how you can use them.

> blanket   bottle   helmet   jacket   map
> MP3 player   smartphone   soap   toothbrush   towel

> I want to bring a bottle. I can use it to carry water.

Song

1 Listen and read. What's your favourite thing in the whole world? 🎧 TR: 55

Now it's mine!

Look at the scarf I'm wearing today.
My great-grandad wore it to keep him warm.
Then he gave it to my grandad.
He gave it to my mum.
And now it's mine!

Chorus
It's my favourite thing in the whole world.
It's my favourite thing in the whole world.
I must look after it well.
Who's going to have it next?

Look at the umbrella I'm using today.
My great-grandma used it to keep her dry.
Then she gave it to my uncle.
He gave it to my dad.
And now it's mine!

Chorus

Look at the bracelet I'm wearing today.
My grandma wore it to give her luck.
Then she gave it to my aunt.
She gave it to my mum.
And now it's mine!

Chorus

2 Listen and sing. 🎧 TR: 56 and 57

3 Sing and act. 🎧 TR: 58

VALUE Look after your things.
Workbook, Lesson 6

1 **Read the invitation. Would you like to go to this party?**

Dear Freya

Please come to my party! It's a pizza, film and sleepover party!

Date: 20th and 21st February

Time: 5.30pm on Saturday to 11am on Sunday

Place: 63 Lakeside Road (It's next to the library.)

Remember to bring: pyjamas, a toothbrush (and your favourite teddy if you want!)

On Friday evening, we're going to eat pizza and watch a film. In the morning, we're going to play tennis, so bring shorts and trainers with you too! You don't need a racket. You can use one of mine.

Text Helen (my mum) to say if you can come. Her number is 07700 900368.

I hope you can come!

Sarah

2 **Read. Then look at the invitation again and answer the questions.**

An **invitation** asks you to come to a party or a celebration. It includes:
- who the invitation is for and who it is from
- what kind of party it is
- the date and time
- the place
- any other important information.

1 When is the party?

2 Where is the party?

3 Who is the invitation for?

4 Who is the invitation from?

3 **Writing skill** Times, dates, addresses

a **Read.**

Time: use *am* (morning) or *pm* (afternoon or evening).

Date: write *st, nd* or *th* after the numbers.

Address: write the number of the house first and then the name of the street or road.

b **Underline and correct the mistakes on this invitation.**

Please come to my party!

It's a costume party!

Date: 10st March

Time: 11.30pm before lunch

Place: Ship Street, 34

4 **Think about a party you'd like to have. Write an invitation for a friend.**

1 Watch the video. Which country has these special clothes? ▶ Video 7

1 Morocco ☐   2 Saudi Arabia ☐   3 Vietnam ☐

2 Watch the video again. Tick (✓) the clothes that you hear. ▶ Video 7

pockets ☐	hat ☐	dresses ☐	trousers ☐
sunglasses ☐	shoes ☐	coat ☐	scarves ☐

3 Circle the correct answer.

1 A 'gandoura' *has / hasn't* got pockets.

2 A 'shesh' is usually *colourful / black*.

3 People wear rice hats to *protect them from the sun and rain / keep their heads warm*.

4 The traditional 'ao dai' dress is *colourful / white*.

5 A 'thobe' has *long / short* sleeves.

6 'Shemaghs' are *always / sometimes* red and white.

4 Work in pairs. Discuss the questions.

1 What special clothes do people wear in your country?

2 What do these clothes look like? When do people wear them?

3 Do you like to wear special clothes? Why? / Why not?

Can I help you?	Yes, please.
I'm looking for a striped shirt.	
How much is this jacket?	**It's** 120 euros.
What size are you?	Small./Medium./Large.
Here's a lovely dress.	**I'll take** it!

1 **Listen and complete.** 🎧 TR: 59

Customer: Good afternoon!

Shop assistant: Hello. Can I help you?

Customer: Yes, please. I'm looking for a new ^{1}_____ .

Shop assistant: What colour do you want?

Customer: ^{2}_____ , please.

Shop assistant: OK. Here's a nice ^{3}_____ .

Customer: Ooh, I like it. It's very nice.

Shop assistant: Great. What size are you?

Customer: ^{4}_____ .

Shop assistant: Perfect! Here you are.

Customer: I'll take it! Oh, but wait. How much is it?

Shop assistant: It's ^{5}_____ euros.

Customer: Oh, that's very expensive!

2 **Listen, check and repeat.** 🎧 TR: 60

3 **Complete the mini dialogues.**

1 Shop assistant: _____ .
   Customer: Yes, please. I'm looking for a new hat.
2 Customer: _____ .
   Shop assistant: It's 50 euros.
3 Customer: I'm looking for brown shoes.
   Shop assistant: _____ .
   Customer: I'm size 39.

4 **Role-play a dialogue between a shop assistant and a customer.**

Hang Son Doong

This video is about a cave in Vietnam, called Hang Son Doong. It's the largest cave in the world. There's a fast river inside the cave too. The cave is more than five kilometres long. In two places, the top of the cave fell in many years ago. So, the sun shines in and trees and plants grow there. Some of the largest stalagmites in the world are here too. Stalagmites are long rocks that point up from the floor of the cave. Some of these are about 70 metres tall.

1 **Read about the biggest cave in the world. Answer the questions.**

   1 How long is the Hang Son Doong cave?

   2 Why are there many plants and trees growing in the cave?

2 **Watch the video. Circle the correct answer.** ▶ Video 8

   1 Ho Khanh could see *water / clouds* coming from the cave.

   2 Hang Son Doong means *Mountain River Cave / Long Beautiful Cave*.

   3 The cave is *18 / 3* million years old.

   4 Some parts of the cave are 200 *metres / kilometres* tall.

   5 It takes about *three / five* days to walk from the road to the entrance of the cave.

3 **PROJECT** Work in pairs. Make a cave.

Make a model of a cave with stalagmites and stalactites. Use black and grey paper, scissors and glue.

4 Find out about an interesting cave. Tell the class about it.

This cave in Spain is very old. It has paintings on the wall.

1 Read, choose and write.

> bridge   island   plain   pockets   sunglasses   waves

1 without a design (e.g. not spotted or striped) _____
2 You walk on this to go across a river. _____
3 This is land that has water all around it. _____
4 The lines of water that move on top of the sea. _____
5 These are on clothes and you can keep things inside them. _____
6 You wear these to protect your eyes from the sun. _____

2 Where does each person want to go? Listen and write a letter in each box. 🎧 TR: 61

1 Eva ☐   2 Carlos ☐   3 Sofia ☐   4 Harry ☐

3 Write answers with a possessive pronoun.

1 Whose striped socks are these?   _They're mine._ (I)
2 Whose plain red shirt is this?   _____ (she)
3 Whose shoes are these?   _____ (they)
4 Whose striped shirt is this?   _____ (he)
5 Whose spotted socks are those?   _____ (we)

4 Write sentences about these topics using these adjectives.

• Sports   • Food   • Books   • Films

> best   worst   more interesting   more popular   most difficult

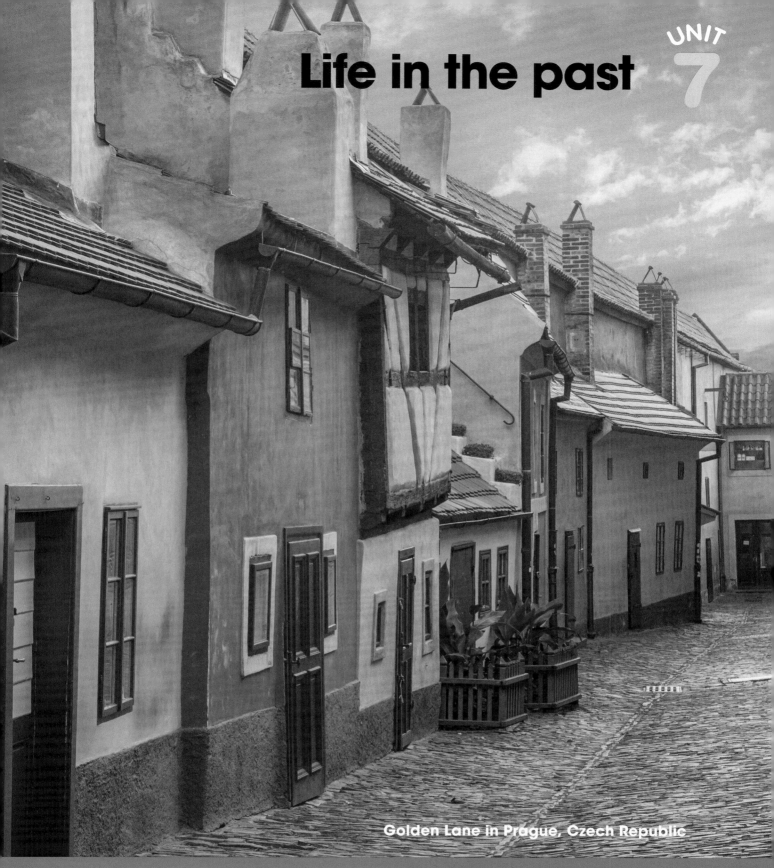

Life in the past

Golden Lane in Prague, Czech Republic

Look at the photo. Answer the questions.

1 What do the buildings look like?

2 How old do you think they are?

3 Who do you think lives here?

Words

1 Listen and repeat. 🎧 TR: 62

the back

the front

an entrance

a floor

a gate

a key

a lift

a roof

downstairs

upstairs

2 Which words from Exercise 1 can you see in the picture?

3 Listen to a talk about ancient Egyptian houses.
Write **T** (true) or **F** (false). 🎧 TR: 63

1 The house in the picture belonged to a rich Egyptian family.

2 The animals slept in a room downstairs.

3 Upstairs, the windows were small because the sun was very hot.

4 The family had meals on the roof.

5 Some families had houses with three floors.

6 Rich families had big gardens with flowers and vegetables.

1 Listen and read. 🎧 TR: 64

> **Verb + preposition**
>
> think, talk **+ about**   *Last week, we talked about the pyramids.*
>
> go, listen, travel **+ to**   *They went to bed early in the evening.*
>
> look **+ at**   *Today we are looking at Egyptian houses.*
>
> look, wait **+ for**   *They waited for the rain to come.*

2 Complete the sentences with prepositions. Do you know the answers?

In ancient Egypt ...

People didn't watch TV or listen ¹_____ the radio. What did they do in the evening?

There weren't cars or trains. How did people travel ²_____ places far away?

How did they know the time? They couldn't look ³_____ a clock.

Did people wait ⁴_____ the sun to come up before they got up in the morning?

How did people clean their teeth before they went ⁵_____ bed? There weren't toothbrushes in those days.

Did people think ⁶_____ work all the time or did they like to have fun?

3 Complete the questions with a verb and a preposition from Exercise 1.

What was life like in the past? How did people do things? What would you like to find out? Write your questions and post them here:

How did people ¹g_____ _____ different floors in a building before there were lifts?

When there weren't any mirrors, how did people ²l_____ _____ their faces?

How did people ³t_____ _____ other countries before there were planes?

My question is about music: How did people ⁴l_____ _____ music before there were radios?

What about the internet? How could people ⁵l_____ _____ answers to questions without it?

4 Discuss the questions from Exercise 3 in small groups.

> I think they climbed up.

> Maybe they used a ladder.

3 Reading

1 Look at the photo. What game are they playing?

2 Listen and read. 🎧 TR: 65

Playing games outside

Sixty or seventy years ago, many children played games on the **pavement** near their houses. They didn't have video games or watch TV, so they had to make their own games outside. They had fun playing together with their friends. Why don't you try these traditional games too?

Marbles

Children played marbles in Roman times nearly 2,000 years ago! Marbles are small **glass** or clay balls. You usually draw a **circle** with **chalk**. You have to throw your marble to hit other marbles out of the circle.

Hopscotch

This is an old game from Roman times too. In Argentina, it is called 'rayuela' and in Malaysia it is called 'ketingting'. First, you have to draw **squares** and numbers with chalk. Then, you take turns to throw a small stone and hop and jump on the squares.

Elastics

This game started in China in the 7th century. Two children have to stand with a long circle of elastic around their legs. Another child jumps and makes shapes with the elastic using their feet. All the children sing a song at the same time.

3 Read again. Write H (hopscotch), M (marbles) or E (elastics).

1 You don't use chalk. __
2 You play this with small balls. __
3 You usually sing. __
4 The Romans didn't play this. __
5 You have to throw things. __, __
6 You have to jump. __, __

4 Match the words in bold in the text with their meanings.

1 a shape with four sides
2 a round shape
3 Windows are made of this.
4 white stone that you can use to draw
5 People walk on this, next to the road.

1 Listen and read. 🎧 TR: 66

> **Has / Have to**
> She **has to** hop and jump.
> Today, children **have to** be careful.
> **Had to**
> You **had to** draw squares on the pavement.
> They **had to** make their own games outside.

2 Read and circle *has to* or *have to*.

Leapfrog is a fun game. You ¹*has to / have to* play it in the gym or in the playground. Four or five children ²*has to / have to* stand in a line. They ³*has to / have to* bend down and put their hands on their knees. Then, one child ⁴*has to / have to* jump over all the children one by one. He or she ⁵*has to / have to* keep his or her feet off the ground. The other children ⁶*has to / have to* stand still. It's not that easy!

3 Complete the text. Use *has to, have to* or *had to* and these verbs.

> have   make   sit   wear (x2)

How was life different 150 years ago?

Today, if someone ¹_____ a bath, they turn on the tap and hot water comes out. But 150 years ago, people ²_____ hot water on a fire. If you live in a cold country, you ³_____ a lot of clothes when you go out. But 150 years ago, people ⁴_____ a lot of clothes in the house! Most houses had only one room with a fire. People ⁵_____ near the fire to keep warm.

4 How is your life different to your grandparents' life? Discuss with a friend.

> I have to clean my room every Saturday. My grandma had to work in a shop on Saturdays.

VALUE Play outside.
Workbook, Lesson 6

UNIT 7   Life in the past   **73**

Song

1 Listen and read. Is Grandad telling the truth? 🎧 TR: 67

When I was your age

This work is boring, Grandad. Can I go to the park?
It's a beautiful day. I want to play in the sun.
I have to read this school book, but it's just no fun.

When I was your age, there was no time for fun.
I had to milk the cow and I had to clean the lorry!
But, Grandad …
Yes?
We both know that you didn't have a cow!
And we both know that you didn't have a lorry!

This homework's really difficult, and I have to clean my room.
I have to put my clothes away. I have to make my bed.
Please can I play in the park instead?

We did hours of homework. Five of us shared a room!
I had to feed the goat and had to work on the farm!
But Grandad …
Yes?
We both know that you didn't have a goat!
And we both know that you didn't have a farm!

2 Listen and sing. 🎧 TR: 68 and 69

3 Sing and act. 🎧 TR: 70

1 Read the timeline on a school website. What can you learn from it?

- ☐ the history of the school
- ☐ important dates in history
- ☐ school term dates

2 Look at the timeline again. When did these things happen?

1 There was a new gate at the entrance.
2 A library opened.
3 The first school started.
4 There were 3,000 students there.

3 Writing skill Numbers

a Find these numbers in the timeline. How do we write them?

1 a number less than 10
2 three numbers more than 10
3 a year in history

b Complete the text with these numbers.

> 2012   six   22   1958

My building has ¹_____ floors and ²_____ different flats. The building started in ³_____ as an office building. But in ⁴_____ they changed it into an apartment building.

4 Write a timeline about your school or another building that you know.

Ashikaga School

832
The first school probably opened here.

1432
The school opened again. A man called Uesugi Norizane brought many books from other countries.

1550
There were about 3,000 students at the school.

1668
People built the gate at the entrance. It's called Nyutoku-mon Gate. There are two other gates at the school.

1872
The buildings were very old and the school closed.

1915
A new library opened here. It had more than 50,000 books.

1990
People built the school again. They built it like it was in about 1700.

Today
The school is a museum and you can visit it. A visit takes about 40 minutes.

Video

1 Watch the video. Who talks about these things? ▶ Video 9

1 AJ ☐   2 Yurara ☐   3 Aliyah ☐

2 Watch the video again. Complete the sentences about the children's grandparents. Use *had to* and these verbs. ▶ Video 9

> ask   play   save   stand up   study

1 They _____ a switchboard operator to make a phone call.
2 They _____ to turn off the TV.
3 They _____ a lot of money to travel by plane.
4 They _____ school subjects without computers.
5 They _____ together outside without mobile phones.

3 Read and write T (true) or F (false).

1 AJ's grandparents didn't have mobile phones.
2 AJ's grandparents had a TV that was black and white.
3 Yurara's grandpa didn't travel by train very much.
4 Some trains in Japan today travel more than 300 kilometres an hour.
5 Aliyah's grandpa made things from wood.
6 Aliyah's grandma sometimes played computer games.

4 Work in pairs. Discuss the questions.

1 What do your grandparents tell you about life in the past?
2 What was the same or different?
3 How would your life be different 50 years ago?

Fresh food

Large pumpkins at the Botanical garden, New York, the US

Look at the photo. Answer the questions.

1 Do you have pumpkins in your country?

2 What can you make with pumpkins?

3 Is it easy to grow food? What do you need?

Words

1 Listen and repeat. 🎧 TR: 71

broccoli

cereal

a chilli

sweetcorn

a courgette

jam

a lettuce

nuts

olives

a strawberry

2 Read and write words from Exercise 1.

1 It's small and red. It's not a vegetable. What is it?

2 We often make it from fruit and eat it with bread. What is it?

3 It has green leaves. We often make salad with it. What is it?

4 They're small and usually green or black. What are they?

5 It has many small, yellow parts. What is it?

6 It's red or green and it's usually spicy. What is it?

3 Read these facts about chillies. Do you think they are true or false? Then listen and write T (true) or F (false). 🎧 TR: 72

1 Big chillies are usually spicier than small ones. ☐

2 Birds eat the seeds of a chilli because they're not spicy. ☐

3 It's good to eat ice cream after you eat a chilli. ☐

4 An orange has more vitamin C than a chilli. ☐

5 You can make jam from chillies. ☐

6 The worker in the photo is going to count the chillies. ☐

Grammar

1 **Listen and repeat.** 🎧 TR: 73

> **How many / How much ...?**
>
> *How many chillies are there?*
>
> *How much cereal do you have for breakfast?*
>
> We use *many* with countable nouns and *much* with uncountable nouns.

2 **Read the food quiz and circle *many* or *much*. Can you guess the answers?**

1 How *many* / *much* water is there in a courgette?

   A 25%   **B** 60%   **C** 95%

2 How *many* / *much* bananas do people around the world eat every year?

   A 10 million   **B** 10 billion   **C** 100 billion

3 How *many* / *much* seeds does a strawberry have?

   A 50   **B** 200   **C** 500

4 How *many* / *much* did the world's heaviest potato weigh?

   A 5kg   **B** 20 kg   **C** 100 kg

5 How *many* / *much* different kinds of nuts are there?

   A 10   **B** 30   **C** 50

3 **Write questions with *How many* or *How much*.**

> apples   biscuits   bread   cereal
> different vegetables   milk

How much cereal do you eat in a week?

4 **Work in groups of three. Ask and answer the questions from Exercise 3.**

> about (five)   (three) bowls of   (four) glasses of
> (two) bottles of   (three) slices of

How much cereal do you eat in a week?   About five bowls of cereal.

Chilli farm in Xuan'en County, Hubei Province, China

3 Reading

1 Look at the photo. What food can you see on the table?

2 Listen and read. 🎧 TR: 74

Let's grow our food!

Fresh food is healthier than **junk food**, but it's often more expensive. In some towns and cities, people are learning to grow their own fruit and vegetables in community gardens. They share the garden and look after the plants together.

Ana and her 14-year-old daughter Marjorie live in Quito, Ecuador. Every morning, Ana goes to the community garden. Marjorie often goes with her. Ten families work together in the garden. First, they plant **seeds** and they water the plants. They pull out **weeds** and pick the vegetables when they're ready. It's hard work, but they grow lots of food! They eat a lot of the vegetables and they sell some at the market too.

Ana enjoys sharing this garden because it brings people together. The children love working outside and watching the vegetables grow. They are also eating more healthily now. 'I didn't like vegetables before,' Marjorie says, 'but now I like to eat lots of sweetcorn and potatoes. They're delicious and they come from our garden.'

3 Match the words in bold in the text with their meanings.

1 plants growing where you don't want them _____

2 unhealthy food _____

3 food that is natural _____

4 plants grow from these _____

4 Read again. Answer the questions.

1 Where does Ana live?

2 How often does Ana help?

3 Who else works in the garden?

4 What do the families do with the food?

5 What does Marjorie like now?

1 **Listen and read.** 🎧 TR: 75

> **some / any**
> *Are there any vegetables? / Is there any water?*
> *There are some vegetables. / There is some water.*
> *There aren't any vegetables. / There isn't any water.*
>
> **a few / a little / lots of**
> *They ate a few olives / a little fresh food.*
> *They grew lots of courgettes / lots of fresh food.*

2 **Complete the sentences with *a few* or *a little*.**

1 Would you like _____ milk in your tea?
2 For the salad, we need a lettuce, _____ carrots, _____ tomatoes and _____ sweetcorn.
3 They have _____ nuts with their yoghurt.
4 They picked _____ apples and _____ olives.

3 **Read and circle the correct answer.**

> ### How to make a school vegetable garden
> 🌱 Find ¹*some / any / a few* space outside. You don't need ²*a little / lots of / a few* space. Start with a small garden.
> 🌱 Choose plants that are easy to grow. Has your school got ³*a few / a little / much* tools? You can use them to make ⁴*some / any / a little* holes for the seeds. Plant ⁵*a few / any / a little* lettuces and ⁶*a few / any / a little* broccoli too.
> 🌱 Leave ⁷*a little / many / a few* space between the different plants, so that you can walk around them easily.
> 🌱 Take turns with your friends to water the plants. They usually need ⁸*lots of / much / a few* water when they're young.

4 **Make five sentences about you, three true and two false. Use *a few*, *a little* and *lots of*.**

I ate lots of broccoli yesterday.

5 **Work in groups. Say your sentences. Can your partners guess the true sentences?**

Vegetables from the Community Vegetable Garden Project in Quito, Ecuador

1 Listen and read. What dishes do you eat that have vegetables? 🎧 TR: 76

2 Listen and sing. 🎧 TR: 77 and 78

3 Sing and act. 🎧 TR: 79

What have we got?

Let's make a big soup today.
How many pumpkins have we got?
Let's have a look. Oh, we've got lots!
Are there any onions?
Let's have a look. Yes, there are a few!
Let's make a big soup today.

Let's make some pasta today.
How much spaghetti have we got?
Let's have a look. Oh, we've got lots!
Is there any sauce?
Let's have a look. Yes, there's a little!
Let's make some pasta today.

Let's make a fruit pie today.
How many strawberries have we got?
Let's have a look. Oh, we've got lots!
Are there any mangoes?
Let's have a look. Yes, there are a few!
Let's make a fruit pie today.

Let's make a sandwich today.
How much jam have we got?
Let's have a look. Oh, we've got lots!
Is there any bread?
Let's have a look. Yes, there's a little!
Let's make a sandwich today.

VALUE Make your own food.
Workbook, Lesson 6

A family prepares dinner in Astana, Kazakhstan.

Pumpkin soup

Preparation time	Cooking time	Serves
10 minutes	25 minutes	six people

Ingredients
30ml olive oil   1kg pumpkin   150ml cream
two onions   700ml vegetable stock

cut

add

stir

Method

1 First, cut the onion into small pieces. Then, put the oil in a pan and cook the onion slowly for five minutes.
2 Next, cut the pumpkin into pieces and add it to the pan. Stir and cook slowly for ten minutes.
3 Add the stock, some salt and a little pepper and cook for ten minutes.
4 Add the cream and cook for another minute.
5 Finally, use a blender to make the soup smooth.
6 The soup is ready! Serve hot in a small bowl. You can also add some pumpkin seeds, some cheese and some pieces of bread on top.

1 **Read the recipe. Do you think you can make this soup?**

2 **Read the information in the box. Then look at the recipe again and answer the questions.**

> A **recipe** needs to tell us:
> - what the ingredients are.
> - how much time it takes and how many people it serves.
> - the order to do things.
> - how to serve the food.

1 Is it easy to follow the instructions? Why?
2 What does the photo show?
3 Which takes longer: preparing the ingredients or cooking the food?

3 **Writing skill** Commas

a **Find the commas in the recipe. Which commas are used after time words and which are part of a list?**

b **Put commas in these instructions.**

- First put the onions in the pan.
- Next add the carrots potatoes and pumpkin.
- Finally add some milk a little salt and some pepper.

4 **Write a recipe for a soup that you like. Think about the ingredients you need and the order of the instructions.**

7 Video

1 Watch the video. Match the countries (1–3) with the fruit (A–C). ▶ Video 10

1 Vietnam ☐   A mangoes
2 Brazil ☐   B olives
3 Spain ☐   C dragon fruit

2 Watch the video again. Write D (dragon fruit), M (mango) or O (olive).

▶ Video 10

1 It can be red on the outside.
2 It is small and round.
3 It can be green or black.
4 It can be yellow on the outside.
5 It can be white or red on the inside.

3 Circle the correct answer.

1 The dragon fruit has got lots of small, *red / black* seeds.
2 Jessica says that *she / her mum or her sister* prepares the fruit.
3 Marcel says that mangoes are a strange *colour / shape*.
4 Marcel says he usually has mangoes in the *morning / evening*.
5 Pablo says that olives are popular in *the UK / Greece*.
6 Pablo likes the olives with *fish / red pepper* inside.

4 Work in pairs. Discuss the questions.

1 What fresh fruit and vegetables do people eat in your country?
2 What do they look like?
3 Which do you like? How do you eat them?

1 **Play in pairs. Find differences between the two pictures.**

> Here, the man is drinking water, but here, he is drinking orange juice.

2 **Now write sentences to explain four of the differences.
Share them with the class.**

The Wind and the Sun

One day, the Wind said to the Sun: 'There are not many things in this world stronger than us, are there?'

'You are right,' said the Sun. 'But we are strong in different ways.'

'Different ways?' asked the Wind. 'You are saying that because you are weaker than me.'

'Really? Do you think so?' asked the Sun. 'Then let's have a competition to see how strong we are.'

'Good idea,' agreed the Wind.

Far below them, there was a road. And on the road they could see a man walking. He wore a winter coat and a scarf.

'I know,' said the Sun. 'Let's see which one of us can take the coat and scarf off that man.'

'Ha!' said the Wind. 'That's easy for me. I can blow them off him.'

So the Wind blew and blew. The leaves flew from the trees. The animals on the ground were scared. Even the birds were scared.

The man was very cold. 'Ooh,' he said. 'What a horrible day!'

He held his coat. He held his scarf. And he didn't take them off. The Wind blew more. But the man held his coat more. In the end, the Wind was so tired, he had to stop.

Then, the Sun came out from behind a cloud. The Sun was hot. 'Ooh,' the man said. 'What a beautiful day it is now!'

He took off his scarf. The Sun grew hotter and hotter. The man was so hot he took off his coat and sat down under a tree.

'How did you do that?' asked the Wind.

'Ah!' said the Sun. 'I told you, there are different ways to be strong. You can blow the leaves from the trees and you can make the animals scared. But sometimes, when you want people to do things for you, it is better not to force them.'

1 Look at the picture. What's the weather like?

2 Listen and read. What part of the story can you see in the picture? 🎧 TR: 80

3 Answer the questions.

Who in the story ...
1 thinks he is the strongest?
2 has the idea for a competition?
3 thinks he can win the competition easily?
4 is scared of the strong wind?
5 likes hot weather?
6 wins the competition?

4 Work in pairs. How can you do these things? Is it best to use strength or a different way?

1 Open a coconut.
2 Take a piano upstairs.
3 Move a donkey that doesn't want to move.
4 Get all the juice from a lemon.

Glossary

blow to push the air, for example from your mouth

competition a test or game to see who can do something better

force to make a person do something that they don't want to do

1 Read and write.

1 This can carry you from one floor to another floor. l __ __ __

2 This is a green vegetable. It looks a little like a flower. b __ __ __ __ __ __ __

3 It's the opposite of *the front*. the b __ __ __

4 A zero is this shape. c __ __ __ __ __

5 Lots of people eat this for breakfast with milk. c __ __ __ __ __

2 Listen and draw lines. 🎧 TR: 81

Ben   Mary   Jane   Anna

Billy   Sally   Nick

3 Read the text. Choose the correct words and write them on the lines.

We've always got ¹_____ apples at home. Everyone in our family likes them.
Do you know how ²_____ different kinds of apples there are? There are more
³_____ 7,000! Apples are sweet, ⁴_____ fruit and they're usually green
or red. You can ⁵_____ apples from the tree, but you need to wait for them to
be ready. Others are for cooking. You have ⁶_____ cook them with some sugar.
They are often used for cakes and pies. Many people drink apple juice too. You can
⁷_____ around the world and find apple juice in almost every country.

1	a few	much	a little		5	to eat	eating	eat
2	much	many	any		6	to	by	on
3	of	to	than		7	travel	visit	see
4	circle	square	round					

The world of the future

Visitors at the National Geographic Encounter:
Ocean Odyssey in New York, the US

Look at the photo. Answer the questions.

1 What are these people wearing?

2 What are they looking at?

3 How are they feeling? Why?

Words

1 Listen and repeat. 🎧 TR: 82

 app

 charge a tablet

 e-book

 go online

 headphones

 interactive whiteboard

 laptop

 microphone

 VR headset

 wifi

2 Read and write words from Exercise 1.

1 This technology connects computers to the internet. _____
2 We put these on to listen to music. _____
3 A teacher uses this to show things. _____
4 We can read one of these on a tablet. _____
5 This is a kind of computer you can carry with you. _____

3 Listen to the conversation about a robot called AV1. Write T (true) or F (false). 🎧 TR: 83

1 The robot is one of the teachers. ☐

2 The student at home is on holiday. ☐

3 The student moves the robot with an app. ☐

4 The student at home can see through the robot. ☐

5 The student can move the robot's head to speak. ☐

6 Students can take the robot outside. ☐

Students in class with an AV1 robot in Oslo, Norway.

1 Read and listen. 🎧 TR: 84

> **The future with *will***
>
> *The robot **will help** a lot of students.*
>
> *They **won't miss** any lessons.*
>
> **Time expressions with *will***
>
> *One day, we'll have robots in our class.*
>
> *In 2040, we won't have teachers in our class.*
>
> *Fifteen years from now, we'll use virtual reality.*

2 Complete the text with *will* or *won't* and the verbs in brackets.

In the future, maybe we ¹_____ (have) a robot at home. It ²_____ (be) cheap, but it ³_____ (be) very useful. We ⁴_____ (use) it to help us with housework. Maybe it ⁵_____ (clean) the house and it ⁶_____ (make) breakfast, lunch and dinner! It ⁷_____ (help) children with homework, but it ⁸_____ (read) them stories. It ⁹_____ (eat) food, but we ¹⁰_____ (need) to charge it every day!

3 Make sentences about the robot you will have in the future. Compare your ideas in pairs.

1 help me with homework

2 tidy my bedroom

3 cook breakfast

4 go shopping

5 do the washing up

6 take me to school

It'll help me with homework.

4 Work in groups. Think of other things robots will do and discuss.

> I think robots will play football with us.

> Maybe. I think they'll wake us up in the morning.

Reading

1 **Look at the photo of a drone and discuss the questions.**

1 What is a drone? **2** Where do you think it is going?

2 **Listen and read.** 🎧 TR: 85

Flying machines

Drones are machines that we can **control** from the ground. They fly, but they don't have pilots. They can carry cameras or other things. In some places, drones have important jobs!

In Rwanda, there are many hills and mountains. It takes a long time to travel between villages by car, so doctors use drones to get medicine or blood quickly. They **send a text** to people in a medical centre in the middle of the country. The people then prepare a box with the medicine to put on a drone and it flies to the doctors. The drone uses **satellites** to fly to the right place. It **drops** the box and it flies back.

Drones can help wild animals too. In Borneo, scientists want to help and protect the orangutans. They need to study their nests, but the orangutans build them at the top of tall trees. They're difficult to find, so the scientists use drones to fly over the forests and take photos.

Will there be more drones in the future? What will they do?

Glossary

blood it's red and it's inside our body   **nest** where birds and animals live

3 **Match the words in bold in the text with their meanings.**

1 make something do what you want it to do _____

2 a machine that travels around the earth and sends information _____

3 let something fall to the ground _____

4 use a phone to write to another person _____

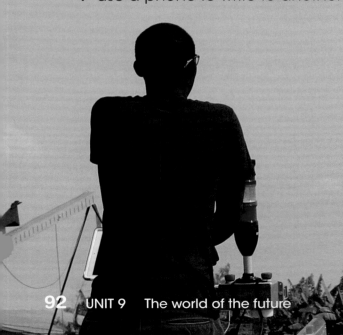

4 **Read again and answer the questions.**

1 Why does it take a long time to travel in Rwanda by car?

2 What do the drones in Rwanda carry?

3 Why is it difficult to find an orangutan's nest?

4 What do the drones in Borneo do?

5 In what other ways will we use drones in the future?

A drone delivering blood is launched near Kigali, Rwanda.

1 **Read and listen.** 🎧 TR: 86

> **Questions with *will***
>
> *Will there be more drones in the future?*
> *Yes, there will. / No, there won't.*
>
> *Where will they fly?*
>
> *What will they do?*

2 **Make questions about the future. Ask and answer with a partner.**

1 there be / flying cars

2 robots / do jobs for us

3 we / use interactive whiteboards in class

4 we / communicate with smartphones

> Will there be flying cars in the future?

> No, there won't.

3 **Think about life 30 years from today. Write four questions.**

> free time   jobs   school   transport

1 Who ＿＿＿＿＿＿＿＿＿＿＿＿＿＿?

2 Where ＿＿＿＿＿＿＿＿＿＿＿＿?

3 What ＿＿＿＿＿＿＿＿＿＿＿＿＿?

4 How ＿＿＿＿＿＿＿＿＿＿＿＿＿?

4 **Discuss the questions from Exercise 3 with a partner.**

> Who will teach children at school?

> I think there will be teachers, but they will have robot helpers.

Let's imagine!

Chorus
What will be different?
What will stay the same?
Will we live in space?
Will the weather change?
No one really knows
How life will be then …
But it's fun to imagine!
Yes, it's fun to imagine!

Will we fly to the moon?
Will we walk in the air?
Will we surf on a dune?
Let's imagine – oh yeah!

Chorus

Will robots play with me?
Will we have purple hair?
Will my phone make me tea?
Let's imagine – oh yeah!

Chorus

Will you be a brilliant artist?
Or a famous tennis player?
Or a doctor or a dentist?
Let's imagine – oh yeah!

2 **Listen and sing.** 🎧 TR: 88 and 89

3 **Sing. Then discuss the questions in the song.** 🎧 TR: 90

VALUE **Use your imagination.**
Workbook, Lesson 6

Control room in Space Camp, Huntsville, Alabama, the US

Writing An opinion text

1 Read the text. What is it about? Tick (✓) the best answer.

1 Facts about school in the future

2 Someone's ideas about school in the future

2 Read the information in the box. Then look at the opinion text again and answer the questions.

> An **opinion text** includes the writer's opinion about a topic and examples of his/her ideas.

1 Which opinion(s) do you agree with?

2 Which opinion(s) do you disagree with?

3 What examples of school trips does Rita give?

3 Writing skill Expressing opinions

a Find phrases in the text that Rita uses to express her opinion.

b Complete the predictions with phrases for expressing opinions.

Sixty years from now …

1 _____ people will eat more fruit and vegetables.

2 _____ most people will drive electric cars.

3 _____ teachers will be robots.

4 _____ people will use VR headsets to play sport.

4 Choose a topic and write an opinion text about the future.

- Food
- Transport
- School
- Sport and games

Sixty years from now, what do you think will be different in schools?

I'm sure that schools will be very different. I don't think there will be pens or paper in the classroom. Students will only have tablets or laptops to send homework and questions to their teacher.

Maybe the teachers will be robots! The real teachers will be at home and they'll see everything through a camera on the robot. I think robots will make the food in the school cafeteria too.

I think students will use VR headsets a lot. Their teacher will take them on virtual school trips every week. Maybe one week they'll go to see the Amazon rainforest and the next week they'll go to the North Pole!

Rita

LESSON 7 Video

1 Watch the video. Tick (✓) the objects you hear. ▶ Video 11

1 computer games ☐
2 robots ☐
3 tablets ☐
4 microphones ☐
5 laptops ☐
6 headphones ☐
7 smartphones ☐
8 VR headsets ☐

2 Watch the video again. Answer the questions. ▶ Video 11

1 What does Marlen use her smartphone for?
2 How does Marlen's brother use his smartphone?
3 Who does Yurara talk to on her tablet?
4 What does Yurara think that everyone will have in the future?
5 Which two school subjects does AJ talk about?
6 What is AJ learning to build?

3 Work in pairs. Discuss the questions.

1 How do you and your friends use technology?
2 Of all of the activities you heard on the video, which is your favourite? Why?
3 How will technology change in the future?

Feeling good!

Boys in Jakarta, Indonesia

Look at the photo. Answer the questions.

1 What are the boys doing?

2 Why do you think they are doing it?

3 What adjectives can you use to describe the boys?

4 Would you like to do this? Why? / Why not?

97

Words

1 Listen and repeat. 🎧 TR: 91

asleep

dark

dry

strong

rest

awake

light

wet

weak

take exercise

2 Answer the questions.

1 How often do you take exercise?

2 When do you feel strong? When do you feel weak?

3 Do you prefer wet weather or dry weather? Why?

VALUE **Sleep well.**
Workbook, Lesson 6

3 Listen to the people talking about sleep. Circle the correct answer. 🎧 TR: 92

1 Sleep helps our body *move* / *get stronger* / *get tired*.

2 Our brain is *slow* / *busy* / *asleep* at night.

3 Young babies sometimes sleep for *12* / *18* / *20* hours.

4 Your room should be *quiet* / *light* / *hot* at night.

5 To sleep better, take exercise *in the morning* / *in the afternoon* / *at night*.

1 **Listen and read.** 🎧 TR: 93

> ***Should / Shouldn't***
> You **should** take some exercise.
> Your bedroom **should** be cool.
>
> You **shouldn't** eat a lot before you sleep.
> You **shouldn't** listen to loud music.

2 **Complete the advice about sleeping with *should* or *shouldn't*.**

1 Your bedroom _____ be very light.
2 You _____ drink fizzy drinks at night.
3 You _____ go to bed at the same time every night.
4 You _____ run and play during the day.
5 You _____ play computer games before you go to sleep.

3 **Complete the advice about getting ready. Use *should* or *shouldn't* and these verbs.**

> drink   eat   forget   go   use

What's your morning routine? You ¹_____ an alarm clock and get up at least 45 minutes before you leave for school. That gives you time to get dressed and have breakfast. You ²_____ to school without eating and you ³_____ something healthy like fruit, bread or cereal. You ⁴_____ fizzy drinks because they have too much sugar. And, of course, you ⁵_____ to wash your face and comb your hair!

4 **Think of advice for people who can't sleep. Then act it out.**

> I can't sleep. What should I do?

> You should count backwards from 100 to 1.

Girl sleeping in Sumpango, Guatemala

Reading

1 Look at the photo. What is the bird doing and why?

2 Listen and read. 🎧 TR: 94

Clean birds

We have a shower every day and wash with **soap** and **shampoo**. We use a **towel** to get dry and we **brush our teeth** with a **toothbrush** and some **toothpaste**. Animals have their own ways of keeping clean.

Some birds have 'dust baths'. They roll on the ground to take off the dirt and insects, and then they shake the dust off their bodies. Most birds also use their beaks to take out dust and insects from their feathers. They use oil from their bodies to clean the feathers too. Birds have about 25,000 feathers so it's not an easy job! But why do they do it? Because it keeps their feathers strong and the oil stops them getting wet.

Oxpeckers are birds that like to clean other animals. They live in Tanzania, Africa and they eat insects from the fur of giraffes. This helps to keep giraffes healthy. Sometimes, the oxpeckers clean the giraffes' ears! They take small pieces of food from between their teeth too. They also clean other animals like zebras, rhinos and buffaloes.

3 Match the words in bold in the text with their meanings.

1 You use it to wash your hands and face. _____

2 You use it to wash your hair. _____

3 You use this to dry your hands and face. _____

4 You should do it twice a day: after breakfast and before you go to bed.

_____

5 You use these to clean your teeth. _____ and _____

4 **Read again. Answer the questions.**

1 Why do birds roll in the dust?

2 How many feathers do some birds have?

3 What do birds put on their feathers?

4 What animals do oxpeckers help, and how?

5 Which parts of other animals do oxpeckers clean?

1 **Listen and read.**  TR: 95

> **Why ...? Because ...**
> **Why** do birds clean their feathers?
> **Because** it keeps them clean and strong.

2 **Match the questions and answers.**

1 Why does a dolphin sleep with one eye open?

2 Why does a lizard stick out its tongue?

3 Why does a kangaroo lick its arms?

4 Why does an elephant have big ears?

5 Why does a cow sometimes lie down in a field?

A Because it helps it to keep warm.

B Because only half of its brain is asleep.

C Because it helps it to keep cool.

D Because it uses it to smell.

E Because they help it to hear and to keep cool.

3 **Put the questions in order.**

1 do / wash your hands / why / a meal / you / before

2 to wash / your hair / use shampoo / why / you / do

3 you / every day / do / change socks / why

4 use toothpaste / do / to clean / you / your teeth / why

5 need / do / why / you / water / to drink

4 **Ask and answer the questions from Exercise 3 with a partner.**

> Why do you wash your hands before a meal?

> Because my hands are dirty. We shouldn't eat with dirty hands.

1 Listen and read. Can you answer the questions? 🎧 TR: 96

2 Listen and sing. 🎧 TR: 97 and 98

3 Sing and act. 🎧 TR: 99

My little brother's questions

Chorus
Why? Why? Why? Why?
He always asks questions
As he walks around the house.
I always try to answer
What life's all about.
Because, because, because, because!

Why do flowers smell nice?
Why are leaves flat?
Why do carrots help you see?
Can you answer that?

Because flowers want the flies and bees.
Because leaves need a lot of sun.
Because Vitamin A is good for your eyes.
You should learn these things – it's fun!

Chorus

Why is it dark at night?
Why is the sun so hot?
Why is the ocean salty?
Do you know or not?

Because the Earth goes round.
Because the sun's a burning star.
Because salt comes from the rocks.
You should learn all this for a start.

Chorus

1 Read the text. Answer the questions.

1 Who do you think is asking for help?
2 Who do you think is giving advice?

Problem

I take a long time to do my homework. I think of other things all the time! Do you have any advice to help me work more quickly?

Advice

Well, here are some tips to help you!

Firstly, you can't work well when you're tired, so you shouldn't work late at night. You should keep your desk tidy, too. Then you can find your pens and books easily. You shouldn't do other things at the same time. You shouldn't listen to music or watch TV and you shouldn't send text messages. It's a good idea to put your phone in another room. You should stop to have healthy snacks, but you shouldn't eat your meals when you are doing your homework.

Good luck!

2 Read. Then look at the text again and answer the questions.

When we write a text to **give advice**, we usually include many different ideas and reasons why.

1 How many different ideas are there in the second message?
2 What reasons does the writer give?
3 Think of two more tips to help someone do their homework more quickly.

3 Writing skill Words that sound the same

a Circle the correct answer.

1 You should brush *you're* / *your* teeth two or three times a day.
2 You should put on a sweater when *you're* / *your* cold.
3 Children shouldn't do *they're* / *their* homework at night.
4 They want to rest because *they're* / *their* tired.

b Think of other words that sound the same but have different spellings.

4 Work in pairs. Choose a question and reply with your advice.

'I'm not sure how to eat healthily. Have you got any ideas?'

'What should I do to keep fit?'

'How can I make friends more easily?'

1 How often do you have a cold? Watch the video to find out what people do when they have a cold in different countries. ▶ Video 12

A

2 Watch the video again. Match the countries and the ingredients used to treat a cold.
▶ Video 12

1 India ☐
2 Morocco ☐
3 Japan ☐

B

C

3 **Read and write T (true) or F (false).**

1 Shiven's grandma can make 'pepper milk'.

2 Shiven puts sugar in his 'pepper milk'.

3 Japanese green tea is called 'umeboshi'.

4 Yurara likes 'umeboshi'.

5 Hasu soup has got garlic in it.

6 Safia likes 'hasu soup' more than 'harira'.

4 **Work in pairs. Discuss the questions.**

1 What do people you know usually do to treat a cold?

2 Is there traditional medicine in your country for a cold? If so, describe it.

3 What do you do when you have a cold or you don't feel well?

Function 3: Requesting and offering help

> Can you carry this bag for me?   Sure. No problem.
>
> Shall I open the door for you?   Yes, please. Thank you.
>
> That's OK.

1 **Read and complete the conversation with your ideas.**

Noah: Hi, Kim. Are you feeling better?

Kim: Hi, Noah. Yes, I'm feeling a bit better.

Noah: That's good.

Kim: It's quite hot in here. Can you ¹_____ for me?

Noah: Sure. ²_____ .

Kim: Thanks.

Noah: Are you hungry? Shall I ³_____ ?

Kim: Oh yes, please. Thank you.

Noah: That's OK. Shall I ⁴_____ ?

Kim: Yes, please.

2 **Listen, check and repeat.** 🎧 TR: 100

3 **Complete the requests and offers of help. Use these verbs.**

> ~~bring~~ bring buy carry close help

1 My coat is upstairs. Can you _____*bring it, please?*_____

2 We haven't got any milk. Shall I _____

3 This shopping is very heavy. Can you _____

4 Are you thirsty? Shall I _____

5 I don't understand this maths question. Can you _____

6 It's cold in here. Shall I _____

4 **Work with a friend. Act out a short conversation using the requests and offers from Exercise 3.**

> My coat is upstairs. Can you bring it, please?

> Sure. No problem.

> Thank you.

Taking photos of lions

You're going to see a video about different ways to take photos of lions. Lions are dangerous animals so it isn't easy to get close to them, especially if they are protecting their cubs. These lions are in the Serengeti National Park in Tanzania, in east Africa. Here, the photographers are using a robot on wheels. There's a camera inside the robot and the photographers control it from far away in a safe place. What do you think the lions will do when they see the robot?

1 Read about photographing lions. Answer the questions.

1 Where do these lions live?
2 How do the photographers take close-up photos of the lions?

2 Watch the video. Read and match. ▶ Video 13

Technology used	Where/When	Results/Photos
1 a robot with wheels	close to the lions	photos of lions walking near water
2 a drone	from above	photos of lions playing together
3 a truck with lights	at night	photos of lions relaxing and sleeping

3 PROJECT **Work in groups. Choose a wild animal.**

Imagine you are taking photos of this animal with a robot camera. What can you see?

THE PANDA IS EATING BAMBOO

THE PANDA'S EAR

THE PANDA'S TUMMY

4 **What did you learn about your animal from the camera? Explain to the class.**

The panda sleeps on its back. It eats a lot of bamboo.

Review 5: Units 9–10

1 Match the opposites.

1	asleep	**A**	dry
2	dark	**B**	rest
3	wet	**C**	light
4	strong	**D**	weak
5	take exercise	**E**	awake

2 Complete the text with the words from the box.

> e-books   headphones   headset
> microphone   online   texts

Most people use their smartphones for more than sending [1]_____ and making phone calls. You can use wifi to go [2]_____ , take photos and use [3]_____ to listen to music. You can record things with the [4]_____ too and use a phone to make a VR [5]_____ . You can read [6]_____ on a phone too.

3 Write sentences about the future. Use *will/won't* and your ideas.

1 On Saturday, I _____ .
2 Next month, I _____ .
3 In the future, robots _____ .
4 In 100 years, people _____ .
5 When I am 50, I _____ .

4 Read and circle *should* or *shouldn't*.

1 Before school, you *should / shouldn't* have breakfast.
2 At school, you *should / shouldn't* talk when the teacher is talking.
3 When you play sport, you *should / shouldn't* always try your best.
4 In the morning, you *should / shouldn't* brush your teeth.
5 You *should / shouldn't* wash your hands before you eat.
6 You *should / shouldn't* eat a lot of food before you do sport.

City life

Night time in Hong Kong

Look at the photo. Answer the questions.

1 What can you see in the photo?

2 Do you know a place that looks like this?

3 Do you live in a town/city or a village?

4 What are your favourite places where you live?

Words

1 **Listen and repeat.** 🎧 TR: 101

airport

bus station

chemist's

fire station

hotel

police station

railway station

restaurant

square

university

2 **Complete with words from Exercise 1.**

Hamburg is the second biggest city in Germany. It has its own [1]_____ so you can fly there easily. Or you can take a train to the main [2]_____. There are many interesting museums and art galleries to visit. It's great for food, too – there are lots of [3]_____ to choose from. Every winter, there is a big market in the [4]_____ near the centre of the city. There are about 100,000 students at 19 different [5]_____ in Hamburg too.

3 **Listen to the information about *Miniatur Wunderland* in Hamburg. Circle the correct answer.** 🎧 TR: 102

1 Frederik first had the idea for the model railway in *2000 / 2002*.

2 Frederik had the idea in a *railway station / shop*.

3 Frederik and Gerrit Braun are from *Switzerland / Germany*.

4 The model railway *is / isn't* finished.

5 There are *more / fewer* cars than buildings.

6 There are *10,000 / 100,000* model trees.

1 Read and listen. 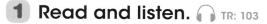 TR: 103

> **Present perfect: affirmative and negative**
> He's *been* to Miniatur Wunderland.
> They've *made* a big airport.
> She *hasn't seen* the airport.
> They *haven't finished*.

2 Look at the notes and make sentences. Use the present perfect.

> ✗ finish the Scandinavia model (Gerrit)
> ✓ build a miniature airport (Frederik)
> ✗ complete the Venice model (Frederik)
> ✗ design a new country (Frederik and Gerrit)
> ✓ start the houses (Frederik and Gerrit)
> ✓ decide on the next city (Gerrit)

Gerrit hasn't finished the Scandinavia model.

3 Complete the conversation with the verbs in brackets. Use the present perfect.

A: ¹_____ you _____ (make) your model town? I ²_____ (finish) mine. Look!

B: That looks great! I ³_____ (not / start) my model. Wow! You've painted yours.

A: Yes, but you don't have to paint it. Look, Kim ⁴_____ (not / paint) hers.

B: I want to put a wall around my town. I ⁵_____ (see) some great pictures. Look at this picture of a town in Italy.

A: My parents ⁶_____ (go) to Italy. I would love to go too!

4 Think about a project you are doing. Talk about what you have/haven't done.

Frederik and Gerrit Braun with one of their train sets

Reading

1 Look at the photo. What can you see in the drawing? Why do you think it's special?

2 Listen and read.
TR: 104

Unforgettable cities

When Stephen Wiltshire was young, he couldn't communicate well. He said his first word (*paper*) when he was five. Then teachers saw that he could draw really well. He loved looking at London and he started to draw the buildings. Stephen has a special kind of memory called a photographic memory. He remembers everything that he sees. It's like a photo in his mind.

Stephen has visited many cities around the world. Sometimes, he flies in a helicopter to see the city. He looks at the **office blocks** and the skyscrapers, the **motorways** and the parks. Later the same day, he starts to draw. He can remember the number of windows, floors and **chimneys** on each building! He has drawn London, Mexico City, Istanbul and New York. In this photo, Stephen is drawing Mexico City. He hasn't finished it, but he has drawn most of the **city centre**.

Stephen has also started to draw 3D pictures. He wears a VR headset and draws the shapes in the air!

Glossary

communicate share information with others

memory the ability to remember

3D with three dimensions

3 Match the words in bold in the text with their meanings.

1 These are tall buildings with many floors. People work here. _____

2 These are big roads. Cars usually drive fast here. _____

3 These are on top of houses. The smoke from a fire comes out of the building here. _____

4 This is usually the busiest part of the city. _____

4 Read again. Write T (true) or F (false).

1 Stephen couldn't speak well before he was five years old.

2 Stephen has a very good memory of what he sees.

3 Stephen hasn't travelled in a helicopter.

4 Stephen can remember the number of floors in buildings.

5 In the photo, he is drawing London.

Stephen Wiltshire is drawing Mexico City.

Grammar

1 Listen and read. 🎧 TR: 105

> **Present perfect: questions and answers**
> *Have you visited a big city?*
> *Yes, I have. / No, I haven't.*
> *Has he travelled in a helicopter?*
> *Yes, he has. / No, he hasn't.*

2 Put the questions in order. Answer them for you.

1 you / a / plane / on / travelled / have
   Have you travelled on a plane?

2 walked / you / up / skyscraper / have / a

3 lion / seen / a / you / have

4 drawn / city / you / have / a

5 a / you / visited / museum / have

3 Make questions to ask about Stephen Wiltshire.

1 visit / many cities
   Has Stephen visited many cities?

2 see / skyscrapers

3 draw / Istanbul

4 finish / drawing of New York

5 draw / 3D pictures

4 Ask and answer the questions from Exercise 3 with a partner.

Has Stephen visited many cities?

Yes, he has.

5 Song

1 **Listen and read. Which of these places would you like to visit?** 🎧 TR: 106

We've moved!

Chorus
We've moved to a new city. Where can we go?
We've moved to a new city. What can we do?

Have you visited the museums?
No, we haven't. What are they like?
There's a lot to see and do.
I can take you, if you like.
Chorus

Have you been to the main square?
No, we haven't. What's it like?
It's the biggest in the world.
It's a wonderful sight!
Chorus

Have you seen the Olympic stadium?
No, we haven't. Is it near?
You have to take a bus,
But it isn't far from here.
Chorus

Have you eaten at that restaurant?
No, we haven't. What's it like?
The food is delicious.
We can eat there, if you like.

2 **Listen and sing.** 🎧 TR: 107 and 108

3 **Sing and act.** 🎧 TR: 109

VALUE **Explore your city.**
Workbook, Lesson 6

Children are walking through a gate at the

1 Look at the poster. Answer the questions.

1 What is the poster about?

2 Where would you see a poster like this?

2 Read the information about club posters. Answer the questions.

A **poster** for a club needs to:

- get your attention.
- explain what the club does.
- give details about when the club meets.
- tell you how to join.

1 How does the poster get your attention?

2 What does the club do?

3 When does the club meet?

4 What do you do if you want to join?

3 Writing skill Using questions to get attention

a **Look at the poster again. How many questions are there? What are they about?**

b **Think about your town/city or village. Complete these questions for a walking club poster.**

1 Have you _____ ?

2 Have you _____ ?

3 Which _____ ?

4 Why _____ ?

4 Work in pairs or groups. Design and make a poster for a walking club in your town/city or village.

How well do you know your city?

Join our Prague walking club!

Did you know our castle is one of the largest in the world?

How old is the famous clock at the main square?

Have you walked across all of Prague's beautiful bridges?

There's more to discover in Prague than you think!

We're a friendly group of families and we've planned some short walks around the city centre. Come along with us! We meet every Tuesday after school. When it's sunny, we sometimes organize picnics on a Saturday afternoon. Bring your family and let's all learn something new about Prague!

Speak to your teacher to find out more.

1 **Watch the video. Match the children with the places they talk about.** ▶ Video 14

1 Safia ☐
2 Marlen ☐
3 Indiphile ☐

A

B

C

2 **Watch the video again. Match the cities (1–3) with two things you hear about them (A–F).** ▶ Video 14

1 Marrakesh A ☐   2 Mexico City ☐ ☐   3 Cape Town ☐ ☐

A It has many markets.
B It is near Table Mountain.
C It has museums and galleries.

D It's a capital city.
E There are many snakes in the square.
F It's by the sea.

3 **Answer the questions.**

1 How many towns in Morocco are bigger than Marrakesh?
2 What can you drink in the square in Marrakesh?
3 What was Teotihuacan?
4 Who in Marlen's family lives in Mexico City?
5 What is Lion's Head?
6 How can you travel to Table Mountain?

4 **Work in pairs. Discuss the questions.**

1 What's the most popular city in your country? Where is it?
2 Why do people go there?
3 Have you ever been there? What did you do?

You can do this!

Climbing wall in Singapore

Look at the photo. Answer the questions.

1 What are these people doing?

2 What's it like to be there?

3 Would you like to do this? Why? / Why not?

Words

1 Listen and read. 🎧 TR: 110

Dan Raven-Ellison was a geography teacher but now he's an explorer. He wants to protect our parks and our green places in cities and the countryside. In 2013, he thought of 125 challenges to do outside with his son, Seb. Here are some of them:

- **crawl** through an old mine
- **discover** a secret cave
- **go kayaking** in the sea
- **go gliding**
- **go snorkelling** in a river
- **go horseriding** in the hills
- **jump off** giant steps
- **smell** the city
- **swing** across a river
- **taste** different ice creams

2 Complete the sentences with words from Exercise 1.

1 We _____ with our noses.

2 We _____ food with our tongues.

3 I can't _____ this wall. It's too high.

4 People _____ new plants in the rainforest every year.

5 My cousin's got a horse. He often _____ in the hills.

3 Listen to the interview with Seb Raven-Ellison. Write T (true) or F (false). 🎧 TR: 111

1 Seb and his dad did all the challenges in nine months. ☐

2 They played football in the sea. ☐

3 They went kayaking in the sea in Scotland. ☐

4 The sheep was standing on the grass. ☐

5 They took the sheep onto the kayak. ☐

6 Seb went down a long zipline. ☐

Glossary

zipline   cliff

1 **Listen and read.** 🎧 TR: 112

> **Present perfect: *ever***
>
> *Have you ever done* something dangerous?
> Yes, I *have.* / No, I *haven't.*
>
> *Has she ever crawled* through a tunnel?
> Yes, she *has.* / No, she *hasn't.*

2 **Make questions for the answers 1–5. Use the present perfect and *ever*. Listen and check.** 🎧 TR: 113

1   *Have you ever climbed a mountain?*
    Yes, I have. I climbed up the highest mountains in England, Scotland, Wales and Northern Ireland.

2   _____
    Yes, I have. I went gliding in the UK and we did a loop the loop.

3   _____
    Yes, I have. One time, we camped on the beach and our tent nearly blew away!

4   _____
    Yes, I have. I went on a boat trip and I saw hundreds of seals.

5   _____
    No, I haven't been to the North Pole. I'd like to one day!

3 **Write four more questions with *Have you ever ...?* to ask Seb.**

4 **In pairs, act out an interview with Seb. Ask and answer the questions from Exercise 3.**

Have you ever been snowboarding?

No, I haven't. I've been skiing, but I haven't been snowboarding.

3 Reading

1 **Look at the photo. Where are the children? What are they doing?**

2 **Listen and read.** 🎧 TR: 114

Exploring the Galápagos Islands

Some children have travelled to the Galápagos Islands as National Geographic Global Explorers. The islands are in the Pacific Ocean. These children have seen many different animals and they've learnt new **skills**. *Sophie Lenoir is from Switzerland and she's nine years old. She told us about her experience in the Galápagos Islands.*

There were sea lions on all the beaches along the **coast**. It was amazing! I saw a humpback whale for the first time. It jumped and **splashed** its tail. One day, we went to Genovesa Island. There were thousands of sea birds all around me. They didn't **hide**. We could see them really easily. My favourite was the red-footed booby. It had a blue beak and red feet.

Another day we went to Española Island and we saw an albatross. This bird is more than two metres from the end of one wing to the other. That's huge!

I learnt how to drive our ship, *Endeavour II*. I drove it across the Equator. It was very exciting. We also saw many kinds of fish. My favourite was the parrot fish. It's got a mouth like a parrot's beak. I learnt so much about our beautiful planet. I'd love to go back there one day.

3 **Read the text again. Answer the questions.**

1 Where were the sea lions?
2 Which animal had a blue beak?
3 What bird did Sophie see at Española Island?
4 What did Sophie learn to do on the trip?
5 Why is the parrot fish called *parrot fish*?

4 Complete with the words in bold from the text.

My name's Aman and I'm 12. We went to an island called North Seymour. There were many iguanas on the rocks by the ¹_____. I learnt some new ²_____ too. I learnt how to swim with the animals! We swam with sea lions. They ³_____ around. They were so cute! But my favourite animals were the giant tortoises. They were so big! My sister and I could ⁴_____ behind one of them easily.

Two young explorers with a giant tortoise on Santa Cruz Island, Galápagos

Grammar
LESSON 4

1 Listen and read. 🎧 TR: 115

Present perfect or past simple?

We use the present perfect to talk about our experiences in the past in general.
She's seen a dolphin.

We use the past simple when we know __when__ something happened.
Yesterday, I went snorkelling.

2 Complete. Use the present perfect and the past simple.

1 _Have you ever walked_ a long distance? (you / walk)
Yes, we have. _We walked_ ten kilometres in Scotland last year.

2 _____ ? (he / go kayaking)
Yes, he has. _____ in the sea in May.

3 _____ rocks? (they / jump off)
Yes, they have. _____ last month.

4 _____ a whale? (she / see)
Yes, she has. _____ last summer.

5 _____ through a tunnel? (you / crawl)
Yes, I have. _____ at school on Sports Day.

3 Make questions. Use the present perfect.

go   go gliding   make   taste   see

4 Ask and answer your questions with a partner. Give more information.

Have you seen a tiger?   Yes, I have. I saw a tiger in a zoo last year.

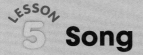

Song

1 **Listen and read. Which challenges would you like to try?** 🎧 TR: 116

Twelve challenges

At the start of the year,
I said to my brother
'Let's do a challenge every month.
We can do it together.'

Chorus
Now it's the end of the year.
We've done twelve challenges.
We've jumped and we've explored!
We've discovered new things!

In January, we went horseriding.
In February, we climbed rocks.
In March, we searched for sea shells.
In April, we made clocks.
Chorus

In May, we learnt to juggle.
In June, we followed a map.
In July, we picked strawberries.
In August, we made jam.
Chorus

In September, we went canoeing.
In October, we jumped the waves.
In November, we swam in rivers.
In December, we explored a cave.
Chorus

VALUE **Challenge yourself.**
Workbook, Lesson 6

2 **Listen and sing.** 🎧 TR: 117 and 118

3 **Sing and act.** 🎧 TR: 119

Afghan girls are practising in Kabul during the Afghanistan Juggling Championship.

1 Read the survey and the report. Answer the questions for you.

2 Look at the survey again. Answer the questions.

  1 What verb form does the student use for the questions?

  2 How many irregular verbs can you find?

  3 What question would you add as question 8?

3 **Writing skill** Expressing quantity

  a Look at the report again. Put these phrases in order, from the smallest number to the biggest.

☐ only one person
☐ three out of eight people
☐ everyone
☐ no one
☐ half of the people

  b Complete the report for the missing activities.

  1 ✓ _____ blue food. (eat)
  2 ✓ ✓ ✓ ✓ _____ a mountain. (climb)

4 Do your own survey. Write five questions and ask six people. Then write your report.

My survey

I asked eight people about their experiences. I used these questions:

1 Have you ever been surfing in the sea?
   ✓ ✓ ✓

2 Have you ever played the drums? ✓

3 Have you ever eaten very spicy food? ✓ ✓

4 Have you ever travelled by helicopter?

5 Have you ever made an animated film? ✓

6 Have you ever spoken English outside of class? ✓ ✓ ✓ ✓ ✓ ✓ ✓ ✓

7 Have you ever slept in a tent on a beach?
   ✓ ✓ ✓ ✓

My report

I counted the Yes answers and here are my results:

- No one has travelled by helicopter.

- Only one person has played the drums and one person has made an animated film.

- Two out of eight people have eaten very spicy food (chillies!).

- Three out of eight people have been surfing in the sea.

- Half of the people have slept in a tent on a beach.

- Everyone has spoken English outside of class!

Video

1 Watch the video. Match to make sentences. ▶ Video 15

1 Lara	has ridden a camel.
2 Kaitlyn	has done kitesurfing.
3 Pablo	has flown in a balloon.

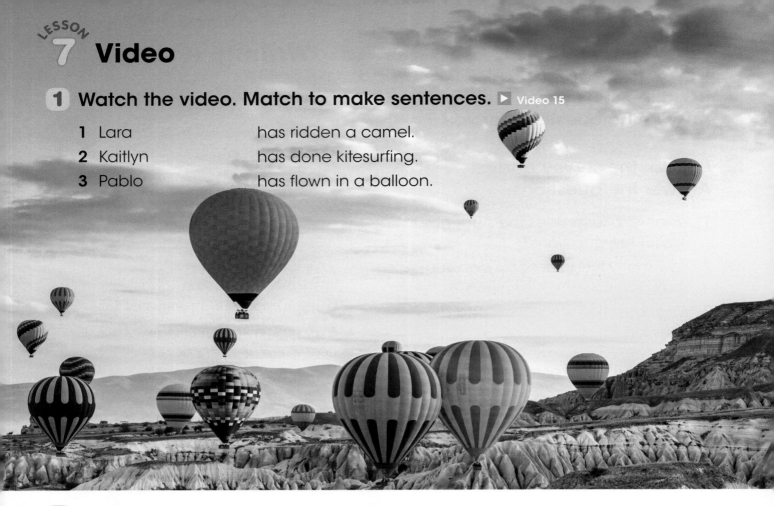

2 Watch the video again. Who talks about each topic? Write L (Lara), K (Kaitlyn) or P (Pablo). ▶ Video 15

1 rocks   **4** town

2 dunes   **5** desert

3 mountain

3 Circle the correct answer.

1 Lara *is a bit scared of / loves* flying.

2 Lara went with *two / three* people from her family.

3 Kaitlyn went to the Gobi Desert *yesterday / last year*.

4 The *wind / sand* in the mountain makes a sound.

5 Pablo learnt to kitesurf *on his own / with a teacher*.

6 Pablo wants to *go faster / jump high* next time he does kitesurfing.

4 Work in pairs. Discuss the questions.

1 Have you ever done something challenging? What was it?

2 What was the experience like?

3 Think of a challenge to set yourself. Why have you chosen this?

1 Read and tick (✓) the correct answer.

1 Hamburg is the ___ city in Germany.
- ☐ biggest
- ☐ second biggest
- ☐ smallest

2 Frederik and Gerrit Braun have worked on the model city of Hamburg. They are ___ .
- ☐ father and son
- ☐ brothers
- ☐ cousins

3 The first word that Stephen Wiltshire said was ___ .
- ☐ *pencil*
- ☐ *paper*
- ☐ *pen*

4 Stephen Wiltshire has a ___ memory.
- ☐ photographic
- ☐ digital
- ☐ short

5 Seb Raven-Ellison did ___ challenges in nine months.
- ☐ 75
- ☐ 100
- ☐ 125

6 In one of his challenges, Seb tasted ___ .
- ☐ tropical fruit
- ☐ ice creams
- ☐ milkshakes

7 A red-footed booby's beak is ___ .
- ☐ green
- ☐ red
- ☐ blue

8 You can see giant ___ on the Galápagos Islands.
- ☐ penguins
- ☐ tortoises
- ☐ dolphins

2 Listen and check. 🎧 TR: 120

The man who wanted a simple life

There was a man from a hot country. He lived in a big city with factories and shops and tall buildings. One day he said, 'I have made my home here. I have bought everything I want. But I don't need all these things. I want to have a simple life.'

So he left his home and all his things and went to live in the forest. He took one thing with him. It was a piece of cloth to wear. In the forest, he built a small hut and for a few months he was happy.

But there were rats in the forest. 'That's OK,' said the man, 'I will get a cat'. And he did. But the cat wanted milk. 'That's OK,' said the man, 'I will get a cow'. And he did. But he did not know how to look after the cow. 'That's OK,' said the man, 'I will get a boy to look after the cow'. And he did. But the boy didn't have a place to live. 'That's OK,' said the man, 'I can build a small house for him.' And he did. 'But who is going to clean my house?' said the boy. 'It's OK,' said the man, 'I will get a maid'. And he did. And soon some of her friends came too. And so they built more houses. In this way a little town grew up.

And the man said, 'What has happened? I wanted to leave my busy life, but it has followed me here!'

Glossary

simple not difficult, not busy

cloth a piece of material

rat a big mouse

maid a girl who helps with the housework

follow come or go after

1 Look at the picture. What things are there in this place, do you think? Tick (✓), cross (✗), or put a question mark (?).

a factory ☐	fruit trees ☐
a railway ☐	tall buildings ☐
fields ☐	a bicycle ☐
a river ☐	a car ☐
a TV ☐	a cow ☐

2 Read and listen. Is the man happy at the end of the story? Why? / Why not? 🎧 TR: 121

3 Put the story in order.

☐ **A** He moved to the forest and built a little house.

☐ **B** But after a time he needed more things.

☐ **C** He had many things, but he didn't like his life.

☐ **D** First he had to get a cat, then a cow, then a boy, then a maid.

☐1☐ **E** A man lived in a busy city.

☐ **F** And so, he had a busy life again.

☐ **G** At first, he was happy in the forest.

4 Write. Then talk about your answers in pairs.

Three things you *have* to have in your life: _____ , _____ ,
_____

Three things you *like* to have in your life: _____ , _____ ,
_____

Review 6: Units 11–12

1 **Look, read and write. Then write two more sentences about the picture.**

1 The restaurant is between the police station and the _____ .

2 There are two girls in the river. One girl is snorkelling and the other is

_____ .

3 What is the boy in the yellow T-shirt doing? _____ .

4 What is the girl in blue trousers doing? _____ .

5 _____

6 _____

2 **Complete the conversation with the verbs in brackets. Use the present perfect or the past simple.**

Milly: I ¹_____ (go) to see a really good film yesterday.

Harry: Really? What ²_____ (be) it about?

Milly: Challenges. It was called *The Big Challenge.* ³_____ (you / see) it?

Harry: Yes, I have. I ⁴_____ (see) it on Wednesday. It was great.

Milly: Yes, I ⁵_____ (love) it too. After the film, we ⁶_____ (visit) my grandmother. She lives near the cinema.

Harry: Oh, I ⁷_____ (meet) your grandma. She works in the school office.

Milly: Yes, that's right. She ⁸_____ (start) the job last month.

1 **Find your favourite photo in the book. Why do you like it? Talk about it with a partner.**

> I think this is the best photo in the book!

> Yes, I like it too. Why do you like it?

> The bird is helping to clean the giraffe's teeth. It's a really funny photo.

2 **Make a list of the following. Then work in pairs. Compare your lists.**

- three interesting facts that you've learnt from this book.
- three people from the book who you would like to meet.
- three activities in the book that you would like to do.

3 **Choose one of the following to do on your holiday.**

- Make a short animated film! Use the advice in Unit 1. Show it to your friends and explain how you made it.
- Research a famous sports person. What did they do when they were younger? Why were they important in their sport? Find out some interesting facts about them.
- Design some holiday clothes. Draw them as a poster and write about them, too.
- Write some challenges for you to do outside with your friends or family. Take photos and write about your experiences.

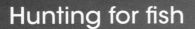

Hunting for fish

People in different parts of the world eat different kinds of food. You're going to see a video about some people, called the Bajau people, who live on the coast of Borneo. Borneo is a big island in southeast Asia. The Bajau people live in small houses above the water. The houses have long wooden legs. The people have small fishing boats and they find most of their food in the sea. They sometimes eat seaweed and many different kinds of fish.

1 **Read about life in Bajau. Answer the questions.**

1 Where do the Bajau people live?

2 What kind of food do they eat and where does it come from?

2 **Watch the video. Write T (true) or F (false).** ▶ Video 16

1 Matthieu Paley is a photographer. ☐

2 The Bajau people cook the food on their boats. ☐

3 Eating seaweed is good for your skin. ☐

4 The Bajau people eat the outside part of the sea urchins. ☐

5 The man in the video catches an octopus ☐

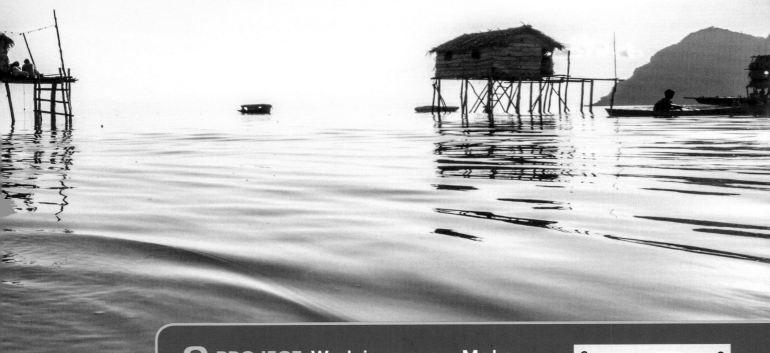

3 **PROJECT** Work in groups. Make a poster.

Research another small island in the world. What do the people eat? Show it on a poster.

4 **Talk to the class about your poster.**

The people in Santorini grow a lot of beans, cucumbers and tomatoes.

FOOD IN SANTORINI, GREECE

TOMATOES

BEANS

CUCUMBER

Annie takes a challenge

In the US, 100 years ago, women usually stayed at home with their families and men went to work. Women certainly didn't go exploring, but Annie Londonderry decided to do just that! Annie was born in Latvia in about 1870. She moved to Boston in the US when she was 18 and she married and had three children.

There's a story that two rich businessmen were in a restaurant together. Annie could hear them.

'These days,' one of them said, 'a woman can do everything that a man can.'

The other man didn't agree with him.

'Thomas Stevens cycled round the world in 15 months and he earned 5,000 dollars too. A woman couldn't do that.'

'I'm sure a woman could,' the other man said. Annie told them she was ready for the challenge!

So, a bicycle company gave Annie a bike. People put adverts on her bike and gave her money. Annie had to leave her children at home with her husband. This was very unusual for a woman in those days. First, Annie cycled from Boston to New York and then Chicago. She thought her bike was too heavy, so she bought a lighter one. She changed her clothes too! Her dress wasn't comfortable so she wore trousers instead.

Back in New York, Annie carried her bike onto a ship, and travelled across the Atlantic Ocean to France. In the south of France, Annie got on a ship to Japan. She stopped in Egypt, Vietnam and China too. And from Japan, she travelled by ship again, back to the US. She was very popular and many people came to watch her pass by. More people gave her money. She sold photos, scarves and handkerchiefs too!

Exactly 15 months after she started, Annie returned home to Boston. And she had more than 5,000 dollars. What an achievement!

Glossary

businessman a man who owns or works in a company

dollar money used in the US

advert information that tries to make people buy something

handkerchief a square piece of cloth that you use to clean your nose

1 Look at the woman in the picture. Why do you think the people are looking at her?

2 Listen and read. Did Annie complete her journey?

🎧 TR: 122

3 Read again and answer the questions.

1 What did the two businessmen disagree about?

2 Why did Annie change her bike and her clothes?

3 Name five different countries she visited.

4 How did she earn some money during her journey?

5 Did she ride her bike all the way round the world?

4 Work in pairs. Discuss the questions.

1 Do you think it was a good thing for Annie to do this challenge? Why? / Why not?

2 Was it fair that she took her bike on the ships? Why? / Why not?

3 Why would it be easier to do the challenge today?

4 Would you like to do this challenge? Why? / Why not?

1 Play in two teams of two.

Instructions: Take turns to throw a die and move around the board. Do the colour challenge to win a point.

→

The Red Challenge

Choose a photo and say a definition for your partner to guess. They have one guess only. Choose a different photo each time.

The Blue Challenge

Roll the die again. Read the challenge that matches your number (1–6). You have 20 seconds to complete the challenge.

1 Find four different countries in the book.
2 Find four activities in the book that you have both done this year.
3 Without looking at the book, sing the chorus of one of the songs. Can you remember it?
4 Find four different kinds of transport in the book. What are they?
5 Find an example of the present tense and the past simple tense.
6 Find an example of the present perfect tense and a future tense.

The Green Challenge

The other team chooses a challenge for you! Choose a different challenge each time.

1 Stand on one leg and say the alphabet.
2 The other team chooses a word for you to spell.
3 Name ten animals in 15 seconds.
4 Count backwards from 20–1.
5 Name ten fruit or vegetables in 15 seconds.
6 Sing a song in English.
7 Ask and answer a question with your partner.
8 Name ten things that you usually take on holiday. You have 15 seconds.
9 Say five irregular past simple verbs.
10 Tell a short story (no more than 30 seconds).

The Yellow Challenge

Look and mime a word or phrase for your partner to guess. They have one guess only. Choose a different word or phrase each time.

play party games	play the flute
wear a costume	brush your teeth
go ice skating	rest
play golf	win a prize
buy an ice cream	go snorkelling
play the violin	go horseriding
play the cello	send a text
give presents	frighten another person
play volleyball	take exercise

CREDITS